Unjust in the Much
The Death Penalty in North Carolina

"...and he that is unjust in the least
is also unjust in the much."
Book of Luke
Chapter XVI, Verse 10

"I shall ask for the abolition of the punishment of death until I have the infallibility of human judgment demonstrated to me."

Thomas Jefferson

Edited by
Calvin Kytle and Daniel H. Pollitt

Unjust in the Much
The Death Penalty in North Carolina

A Symposium
to Advance the Case for a Moratorium
as Proposed by the American Bar Association

Chestnut Tree Press
Chapel Hill
An imprint of Seven Locks Press

CHESTNUT TREE PRESS*
Carolina Meadows, V-130
Chapel Hill, NC 27514
919-967-8662

*"Do me justice," says the Chestnut Tree.
—*The Language of Flowers.* London.
Michael Joseph Ltd. 1968.

The sponsor encourages duplication and the widest possible circulation of this book. Bulk orders and requests for permission to excerpt should be addressed to:
Geoffrey Mock
1008 Lamond Avenue, Durham, NC 27701,
or email at: geoff@dukenews.duke.edu

PRODUCED BY CALVIN KYTLE
of Chestnut Tree Press as a contribution
to North Carolinians Against the Death Penalty

Printed and bound by Thomson-Shore, Inc.
Layout and typography by Sean Husick, with the assistance of
Jeff Waag, Kinko's, Chapel Hill.

Manufactured in the United States of America

Library of Congress Cataloging-in-Publication Data
Unjust in the much: the death penalty in North Carolina: a symposium to advance the case for a moratorium as proposed by the American Bar Association / edited by Calvin Kytle and Daniel H. Pollitt.
p. cm.
"Based on the transcript of a symposium...held April 17, 1998 at the University of North Carolina in Chapel Hill."
Includes index.
ISBN 0-92-976568-0
1. Capital punishment — North Carolina Congresses.
I. Kytle, Calvin. II. Pollitt, Daniel H. III. Title.
KFN7965.C2 U55 1999
345.7560773-dc21   99-39961
CIP

Distributed to the trade by Seven Locks Press
P.O. Box 25689, Santa Ana, CA. 92799. (800) 354-5348

To the memory
of Paul Green,
and to every person,
guilty or innocent,
on Death Row.

PUBLISHER'S NOTE: *Unjust in the Much* is the edited transcript of a symposium sponsored by North Carolinians Against the Death Penalty, an umbrella organization of thirteen civic and religious groups opposed to capital punishment. The symposium was held Friday, April 17, 1998, in the Friday Center at the University of North Carolina in Chapel Hill.

Acknowledgments

The symposium from which this book derives was funded by the Paul Green Foundation and the North Carolina Academy of Trial Lawyers. It was planned and arranged by a committee chaired by Dan Pollitt, of the North Carolinians Against the Death Penalty, and Geoffrey Mock, of Amnesty International. Also serving on the committee were Marshall Dayan, of the North Carolina Academy of Trial Lawyers; Chris Fitzsimon, of the Common Sense Foundation; Paul Green III, of the Paul Green Foundation; Deborah Ross, of the American Civil Liberties Union, North Carolina; Lao Rubert, of the Carolina Justice Policy Center; and Gerda Stein, of the Center for Death Penalty Litigation. The Committee is especially grateful to Caroline Weller for help with administration and arrangements.

Publication of *Unjust in the Much* would not have been possible except for generous financial contributions from:

Julius Chambers, Leslie Dunbar, W. W. Finlator, Elise Goldman, Bishop F. Joseph Gossman (Catholic Diocese of Raleigh), the Paul Green Foundation, Eugene Gressman, Tye Hunter, Charles Lambeth, James Megivern, Dan Okun, Daniel H. Pollitt, Mary Norris Preyer (the Ogleby Foundation), Ken Rose, John Rosenberg, the Mary P.B.T. Semans Foundation, Robert Seymour, Dean Smith, Louise and McNeill Smith, Norman Smith, Chuck Stone, Mary Ann Tally, the Peace and Reconciliation Committee of the Watts Street Baptist Church (Durham), the North Carolina Trial Lawyers, and the law firms of Fuller, Becton, Slifkin & Bell and Glenn, Mills & Fisher.

The publisher acknowledges with appreciation the assistance of Alice Garfield, Elizabeth Kytle, and Rebecca Lacy.

*"Besides everything else, capital punishment
is a brutality this beloved North Carolina of ours
should abolish forevermore and soon."*

Paul Green
Author, *The Lost Colony*
Letter to attorney L. Lyndon Hobbs
November 30, 1962

CONTENTS

Unjust in the Much

The Death Penalty in North Carolina

"Why We're Here"

Dan Pollitt, Presiding

*"Whatever you think about the death penalty,
a system that will take life must first give justice."*

So spoke former American Bar Association president John J.
Curtin Jr., addressing a Congressional committee in 1991.

In February 1997, the ABA resolved that the thirty-eight states
whose statutes authorize capital punishment — the states that make
up the so-called "death belt" — impose a moratorium on all executions
until death penalty cases are administered fairly and through
procedures that minimize the risk of executing the innocent. North
Carolina is one of these states.

The Bar Association singled out four principal areas of concern:

1. Adequacy of Counsel. The ABA noted that in some states
"grossly unqualified and undercompensated lawyers...are often
appointed to represent capital clients" with the consequence that the
trials are "more like the flip of a coin than a delicate balancing of the
scales of justice."

2. Proper Process. The same inadequacy of counsel prevails on
appeal where too many inexperienced and/or underfunded attorneys
fail to raise issues of constitutional significance. Consequently, the
federal courts on habeas corpus (post-conviction review) refuse to
consider claims not properly raised in the state courts. When
constitutional issues are properly raised in federal habeas corpus,
some 40 percent of Death-Row inmates obtain relief.

3. Race Discrimination. Defendants are far more likely to get
the death penalty if the victims are white. In Kentucky, about a
thousand African Americans have been murdered over the past twenty
years. Not one of the prisoners on Death Row is there for the murder
of a black.

4. Execution of the Mentally Retarded and Juveniles. The ABA has policies decrying execution of the mentally retarded (as defined by the American Association on Mental Retardation.) It also has policies opposing execution of persons who were under the age of eighteen at the time of the crime. To no avail. As of the last count, mentally retarded prisoners account for between 12 percent and 20 percent of the Death Row population. Since 1973, death sentences have been imposed on 140 juvenile offenders.

The ABA resolution for a moratorium has received little media attention and has gone unheeded by the state legislatures, including our own. The symposium today has been convened in an effort to enlarge public understanding of the issue and its implications for North Carolina, and thereby encourage the General Assembly to act.
***

Not long ago the *Nation* magazine reviewed a book in which the author said he was no longer going to represent people in capital cases because "saving a few lives here or there is outweighed by lending legitimacy to the system." The reviewer asked whether other lawyers felt the same way. Stephen Bright, director of the Southern Center for Human Rights, wrote in and said:

"The small number of capable lawyers who have represented those facing death have not saved 'a few lives here or there.' They have saved thousands of lives. Caring, conscientious, competent lawyers can save lives by providing poor people with the same quality of legal representation that enables wealthy people to avoid the death penalty. Those of us who care about life and about justice cannot end capital punishment at this moment in history, but we can, like those working on the underground railroad before the abolition of slavery, get some people to safe passage, one at a time. We can bear witness to injustices that would otherwise never come to light; we can attempt to shake our fellow citizens out of their complacency about these injustices. It is this engagement with the system that will save lives and bring us closer to the day when the United States joins the rest of the civilized world in making permanent, absolute, and unequivocal the injunction, 'Thou shalt not kill.'"

With this thought in mind, I welcome you on behalf of the North Carolinians Against the Death Penalty. It goes without saying that every member of this audience cares about life and about justice. I ask you all to share your knowledge and your ideas with the caring, conscientious, and competent lawyers, judges, professors, psychiatrists, and clerics who make up our five panels.

Panel I

The Demographics
of Death Row

Frank Ballance, Moderator
North Carolina State Senator, Second District

This is not the most popular place to be today in North Carolina. You know that. But it's significant that we're here discussing the death penalty, for the issue is not simply going to go away. We have to keep talking about it. We have to keep talking about it, and organizing and acting and lobbying, until it's resolved.

Over my lifetime I've been disappointed that it takes so long to turn things around. When I left law school in 1965, I thought I was going to go back to Bertie County and take care of all the problems in a couple of weeks. I should have known better, because I'd had a sign that this simply wasn't going to happen. When I was in my second year of law at Carolina Central, I went to a very prestigious law firm in Windsor, and asked them for a job. And they said, "Business is kind of slow in summer, but by the way there's a colored lawyer over in Edenton. His name is Tillett. Maybe he needs some help." And then I went upstairs to the courtroom, and the courtroom was segregated. Being a defiant citizen of Bertie County, I sat on the "wrong" side. I sat on the "white" side, and the sheriff tiptoed over to me and said "You'll have to move over." I wanted to be defiant, but I also wanted to pass the bar. I chose to walk out.

When I go back to Bertie County nowadays, I'm received very well. There's been a lot of progress. But not nearly enough. Eva Clayton has distinguished herself in the halls of the United States Congress, yet there are citizens in Bertie County today who, simply because of

5

the hue and pigmentation of her skin, are not willing to vote for Eva Clayton.* One of them is the incumbent sheriff.

About the death penalty: I was sitting in my office a couple of days ago and somebody from the North Carolina Department of Corrections walked in and said, "Senator Ballance, we want to get rid of the gas chamber in North Carolina." The reason he gave was that it was stressful on the staff and it was dangerous; it's a small chamber and you can't get a gurney in too well to exit after the person has been put to death and "it would be far better if we just voted for lethal injection."

Now, I'm opposed to the death penalty. But I'm also opposed to lethal injection. I don't think the people of North Carolina like looking at the death penalty. But the easier we can make it, the closer we can get it to euthanasia, the more we can have these deaths at midnight when nobody's watching and you just read about it in the papers the next day — the more we distance people from the realities of executions, the easier it is for them to tolerate the death penalty.

This bill will be coming up in the short session, and for this reason I don't think I want to support it.

As for Death Row--

I live in Warrenton. I grew up in Bertie County — that's in rural northeastern North Carolina. I practice law in three judicial districts. Six A is Halifax County. Six B is Bertie, Northampton, and Hertford counties. Nine is Warren, Vance, Granville, and Person. The population is rather scarce in these counties. Northhampton County has roughly 22,000 people but David Beard, the district attorney over there, has four people on Death Row. Bertie County has 24,000; David Beard,

---

*Among the ways that Eva Clayton has distinguished herself in Congress is with her expressed opposition to the death penalty. "Other steps must be taken to effectively prevent crime and violence," she has said. "Capital punishment is no deterrent; moreover, it violates an individual's guaranteed constitutional rights by inflicting cruel and unusual punishment. The death penalty contains hypocrisy within itself."

this same district attorney, has three on Death Row from Bertie. Beard also represents Hertford County and he has one on Death Row from Hertford County. So — that's eight people that this one district attorney, who represents about 65,000 people, has on Death Row.

The prosecutors have discretion, you know. I didn't use my computer, but I think my numbers are correct. Wake County has nine people on Death Row. Mecklenburg has seven. Buncombe has ten. D. A. Keith over in Winston-Salem, he has eleven people on Death Row from Forsyth County. Robeson County has gone down to five from seven. There's one in Warren County.

I'm not an expert on the death penalty. It must be ten years since I tried a death penalty case, so I would not feel confident trying any one of these cases. But I think there are people trying them who're less competent than I am. And that's bad news.

It would be difficult to "melt down" and pour some of my Senate colleagues in here this morning. This is an election year and it's not popular out on the track to be against the death penalty. That's one of our big problems. But I'm convinced that the people of North Carolina have been misunderstood, to some degree. What they're looking for is the absence of chaos and violence and killing and rapes in their communities. To the extent that we can resolve these issues, the hue and cry for the death penalty will subside.

HENDERSON HILL
Attorney, Ferguson, Stein, Wallas, Adkins, Gresham & Sumter, Charlotte. (Former Director, Center for Death Penalty Litigation)

At the end of March 1998 there were 177 people condemned to death in North Carolina. That is nearly double the size of the state's Death Row when I moved to North Carolina in 1991.

The demographics should not surprise students of the effect of race and poverty on issues of criminal justice. Of the 177 on Death

Row, ninety-six are black males; seventy-one are white males; three are Native American males; four are other males; three are white females. Ten persons have been executed under the death-penalty statute enacted in 1977 — nine white men and one white female. The next person scheduled to be killed by the state is an African American; his execution date is April 24.

Statistics and demographics do not come close to describing the injustice reflected in North Carolina's Death Row. Yes, black males are sentenced to death in disproportionate numbers. Individuals convicted of crimes in poor and rural counties are far more likely to receive a death sentence than persons convicted of similar crimes in more affluent and more urban counties. Almost every individual on Death Row was socially and economically disadvantaged at the time of prosecution. These, however, are macro concepts. The injustice of Death Row is most powerfully described at the micro level, in the case histories of the men and women condemned.

As I scan the audience, I note the presence of several people who are well-positioned to tell the stories of injustice locked away in Central Prison. Steve Edelstein is a lawyer in a two-lawyer office in Raleigh representing one of two young black males sentenced to death for killing another young black male in Hickory. Most people would describe the killing as a "garden-variety" street crime. A young relative told the two condemned men that she had been raped and robbed by an armed assailant. They went looking for the assailant and found him. A gunbattle ensued and the young woman's assailant was killed. In many jurisdictions these facts would not merit a conviction for voluntary manslaughter. Indeed, the lawyers and prosecutors involved thought the case would be settled by plea bargain and would never reach trial, much less a capital sentence hearing. The young men, originally from Philadelphia, did not trust court-appointed counsel and complained about inaction by the local attorneys. The attorney-client relationship deteriorated to actual hostility before trial. The death sentence proved the axiom: "a house divided cannot stand."

Sitting in the back is Joey Morris who, together with his partner Mark Ash (pro bono lawyers from one of Raleigh's largest law firms), represents a black man sentenced to death in one of the poorest and most rural counties in eastern North Carolina. The young man is severely mentally retarded; his IQ registers in the low fifties. Court-appointed counsel did not present any mental health evidence at trial. During the post-conviction investigations even the psychiatrists at the state hospital agreed that this young man is incapable of forming the levels of intent the law requires to impose criminal responsibility. Court-appointed lawyers did not look and therefore did not find this evidence at trial. The young man sits condemned to death.

But Steve and Joey would tell you that race and poverty have much to do with their client's sitting on Death Row. The role of race and poverty is not blatant in the historical sense. The victims in both cases are black, as are all defendants and co-defendants. Geographically one case arose in the rural east while the other occurred in an urban area in the west. All defendants were poor and represented by court-appointed counsel who, by all accounts, did not understand, know, or like their clients. Lawyers like Steve and Joey, who are willing to investigate these cases and raise issues that make them unpopular with fellow members of the bar, the judiciary, and local communities, shine the light of truth on the arbitrary and capricious way the death penalty is imposed in North Carolina. The challenge is to get the courts, the politicians, and ultimately the people of North Carolina, to look for this truth, or at least to be receptive to it.

There are reliable sources of statistical and demographic information about the individuals condemned to death in North Carolina and across the country. The Center for Death Penalty Litigation (CDPL) in Durham monitors very closely the legal status of all individuals on Death Row at Central Prison and the Women's Prison in Raleigh. Similarly, CDPL receives and maintains the quarterly reports published by the NAACP Legal Defense Fund describing the demographic makeup of the national Death Row population.

For me, the case that best demonstrates the unfairness and cruelty of the death penalty is always whatever case I am most recently and most directly involved with. Today, that is the case of Elias Hanna Syriani. In many ways Mr. Syriani does not fit the profile you would expect to illustrate inequity in the capital punishment system. First of all, he's not a young man; this man pushes sixty. He's not black, nor is he white. He's an Arab American, a Palestinian Christian. Mr. Syriani did not get caught in the gun sights of some rural district attorney anxious to exploit another "notch" on his gunbelt at the next election; in fact he lived and was prosecuted in Charlotte. Probably 95 percent of the people charged with capital crimes are indigents represented by court-appointed counsel. Not Mr. Syriani. Mr. Syriani worked steadily for the fifteen years that he lived in the United States and for the thirty-odd years that he lived in Palestine. He was a homeowner and he was able to raise $10,000 to retain private counsel. Many of us familiar with the system recognize that ten thousand dollars is not much of a shield: It doesn't pay for investigation, it doesn't pay for expert services, it doesn't pay for counsel to meet with other lawyers to seek out help and to figure out the best defense. Is it surprising, then, that a legal defense constrained by such a low spending unit would be unable to mount an effective defense?

The argument brought by his advocate was self-defense. His lawyer pounded his fist on the table, over and over again. Self-defense. Self-defense. Self-defense. It was not a defense that went well in Mecklenburg County. The jury had a hard time understanding how this man's wife, who was simply driving her car at 11 o'clock at night, could have been the aggressor. How could this woman, mother of four, have inflicted on him such injury as to justify the response — stabbing a screwdriver into her forehead? The self-defense that the lawyer was advocating so loudly, that his client was right when he killed this woman, just didn't connect with the jury.

Well, the one thing that the jury didn't understand, and the lawyer didn't understand, was that this was a man who thought of himself as a good and decent person, who saw himself as a hard-working Christian. His Catholic faith had taken him through the troubles in Palestine, all the religious discord there. In Palestine he had been a successful worker, a popular entertainer — he was a traditional Arabic singer — a person of some status. His sense of self-esteem was grounded in his ability to provide for his family. And when he came to the United States and settled his family here, he brought with him the traditional Christian-Arabic notions of family — notions of family that would offend many of us. Under this traditional view, the woman's place, the wife's place, is in the home.

What the jury in Mecklenburg did not hear was how this man's view of the world was one that served him well in his homeland and that drove him to good deeds. In the United States that view brought clash and shock of clinical proportions. The jury didn't understand this because the lawyer didn't know. The lawyer didn't care, and the jury didn't find out. If there is one principle that I see in Mr. Syriani's case — a man whose act cannot be justified but whose life should not be taken — is that the forces that led to this crime were not discovered by his lawyer and consequently never explained to the jury.

There's a certain bizarreness that you see in the application of the death penalty in this particular case. The most immediate victims are the four children who were rendered motherless by the crime. Four children who, by all accounts, the father doted on. One son whom he particularly doted on, and the two daughters that he slaved over for twelve and fifteen years. When we talk to the children now, they say what they would have said then; even though the crime cannot be justified, they do not want their father executed. The oldest daughter, who was closest to the mother, who was most Americanized, is still full of anger at her father. But she does not want to see her father killed. The son is now entering adulthood in the Chicago area and has rejected, for the most part, the traditions that were so important to Mr. Syriani. Nevertheless, he wants his father to live.

Is the killing of Mr. Syriani by the state an effective way of communicating the evil of domestic violence? Does it protect the interest of the family? Did Mr. Syriani's jury consider these questions. No, no, and no. Mr. Syriani's lawyer never even interviewed the children before the trial. All four children were put in the care of Mr. Syriani's sister in Chicago. The sister completely supported her brother and wanted only the best for him. She would have been happy to have Mr. Syriani's lawyer talk to the children, find out about their history, find out about their feelings and reactions. The lawyer didn't go. The lawyer never talked with them. The lawyer didn't care. Was it that the $10,000 wasn't enough? Or was it that the lawyer's training and experience just didn't teach him the importance of finding the facts?

Mr. Syriani is different. Perhaps I consider him so because he's my client. I know him much more personally, much more intimately than I know others on Death Row. I am convinced, however, that if we were to run down the list of all the individuals on Death Row, we would find something different in each one of them. It's almost unspeakable that a government, in your name, would seek the execution of Elias Syriani. But they have. They've obtained the death warrant, and as of today's date no court has said no. The courts are saying that any trial errors committed were harmless.

In his opening statement Mr. Syriani's lawyer promised a case of self-defense but later told the jury, "No, we're not arguing self-defense," and in his closing argument said, "Well, it's imperfect self-defense." This lawyer couldn't figure out what to ask the jury to believe, so it is no wonder that the jury didn't understand. A sixty-year-old man who by all accounts lived a life devoted to family now sits condemned to death for a tragic violent explosion ignited by forces beyond his capacity to control. Do the people of North Carolina really believe that putting Elias Syriani to death is necessary and appropriate?

MARSHALL DYAN
North Carolina Academy of Trial Lawyers

People on Death Row in this country, and in North Carolina in particular, are there for a reason that can be identified before they are even tried: People on Death Row are people without means.

Let me assure you that if you ask Henderson or any of the lawyers in this room how much they would charge to undertake a capital defense, a first-degree defense, none of them would say anything less than $75,000 or $100,000 because that's the number of hours it takes to do a capital case correctly. So, for somebody to retain a lawyer for $10,000 who's charged with first-degree murder, that's a man who's not really a man of means. There are no people on Death Row in the state of North Carolina who are people of means. They are all *indigent* people.

I point to one recent example, a case of first-degree murder in Wake County that many of you may be familiar with. A man from Cary, Kenneth Boychuk, was alleged to have pushed his wife off the bridge of the interstate. According to the state, he looked down and saw that she hadn't died, then went down and finished killing her by smashing her head in with a rock or a brick. Now, under the law of North Carolina, if there is evidence to support an aggravating circumstance, as there was in this case, first-degree murderers may not be pled for life sentences. The law was designed in an effort to eliminate arbitrariness. Nevertheless, this gentleman had the means to retain Roger and Wade Smith and all of a sudden, after the guilt phase was almost over, a guilty plea was entered, in exchange for which the prosecution said, "We will not go forward with a proceeding for capital sentencing." It was absolutely against the law, what was done in this case. But who was going to complain? I'm certainly not. I hope none of you in this room is going to complain. The defendant is certainly not going to complain. The state made the deal with him; they're certainly not going to complain. So there's no way for this man's sentence to get reviewed. What happened stands on the record as proof that, in spite of attempts by courts and our legislature to try and eliminate arbitrariness, if you're a person of means in this state you simply will not be sentenced to death, no matter what you do.

I was a young law student in Mississippi in 1983 working for the Mississippi ACLU and its death-penalty project. Shortly after I got there a well-known city councilman named Ed Cates was killed. It was headline news in the *Jackson Clarion Ledger* that he had been in an automobile accident; his car veered off the highway, went down an embankment, hit the bottom of a gully, exploded and caught on fire. Mr. Cates was reported to have been killed. He had a very high-profile funeral. The lieutenant governor was there, and so were the mayor and all the city council.

Well, about seven or eight weeks later disturbing reports began to be heard that Mr. Cates was alive and living in Lawrenceville, Georgia, under the assumed identity of a retired army colonel. He had contacted his wife to get some of the insurance proceeds because the $250,000 that he had taken from a client before he left the state of Mississippi apparently wasn't enough for him to live on in Lawrenceville. She did the right thing. She turned him in, and he was extradited back to Mississippi. It was discovered that he had picked up a hitchhiker, gotten this person drunk, put him behind the wheel of his car, sent the car off this embankment and down into the gully, where the car exploded. This itinerant traveler was either killed by the impact or burned to death.

But Mr. Cates was never tried for murder. He was tried for embezzling the money from his client, but he was never tried for murder. The state said that it couldn't try him for murder because the remains of his victim were burned so badly that he couldn't be identified.

Examples are rampant. I could go on and on about people of means who commit heinous crimes worthy of the most severe prosecution, but it doesn't happen. The death penalty is reserved for poor people. Not only is it reserved for poor people, but most of the time it is also reserved for people who are not from the community in which they're tried. They are people who come into a community. They're traveling around, they commit a murder, and because they are not from the community the jurors don't know them, can't look at this person and say "Oh yeah, I remember his mother, she was a schoolteacher." Or they can't look at the person and say, "Oh yeah, I remember his dad; he was a principal over at the middle school." Because they're not of the community, it's very easy to pass them off as inhuman, something other than human, not one of us.

Let's take a look at a highly publicized case — Susan Smith in South Carolina. She was of that community, and that community could not commit her to death because they knew all of the tragic circumstances that had surrounded her life. She was one of them. In spite of her horrible crime, that community could not take her life. People on Death Row are primarily poor and primarily not from the community in which they were tried and convicted.

Sadly enough, we also know that most of the people on Death Row are there because they've taken the lives of white people. As study after study after study has shown, if you take the life of a white person you're six to ten times more likely to get a sentence of death than if you take the life of a person of color. This may be the saddest of all the statistics. For what does it say about us as citizens? It says that when we serve as jurors we still place greater value on the lives of white people than we do on the lives of people of color.

And, last but not least, better than 50 percent of our clients have serious mental health problems that have been either undetected, undiagnosed, or untreated. We know this simply from the anecdotal evidence. In the twelve years that I have represented Death Row inmates I have never had a client who wasn't the victim of serious abuse or serious neglect as a child, and there's not a lawyer in this room or in this state who has represented Death Row inmates who will tell you otherwise.

The people of this state, the people of this country, simply don't have the stomach for applying the death penalty in a nonarbitrary way, in a way that's across the board and fair. They don't want to do it. They only want to impose the death penalty on those people "who are not like us, who are something other than us." But the bottom line is, there aren't any such people; there aren't any people who are other than us. They're all human.

FAYE SULTAN
Director, University Psychological Associates, Charlotte

I'm not an attorney. I'm a psychologist. I come at this issue from a different perspective.

You'll notice that neither Henderson nor Marshall had the stomach to tell you about the average background of the people who live on Death Row. I'm going to tell you, by using the example of a man who's dead.

I can talk about Ricky Sanderson because he said I could after he was gone. Mr. Sanderson volunteered to be executed, if such a thing is possible, because he simply couldn't stomach himself any longer.

Only three women live on Death Row in North Carolina. I know two of them. They have backgrounds very similar to that of Ricky Sanderson. Ricky's story is their story, too. Tragically, it is also the story of every resident of Death Row, men and women alike. It is the story of a relentless, crushing, and ultimately criminalizing, sequence of inequity and unfairness.

Ricky Sanderson was reared in a two-room house by a mom and a dad who physically fought every day of his life. When the mother could no longer stand the fact that her husband was raping her and beating her in front of the three children, she left and left the three children behind. They were all under eight years old at the time. What Ricky witnessed all through his childhood was the routine raping of his sister on the floor in front of him while he was tied to a bed and forced to watch.

I remind you that one out of three children in our state is seriously sexually abused before the age of sixteen. We talk about that number thing, that statistic thing — let's talk instead about what happens to one little boy, one little boy who has to watch, for the witnessing of sexual violence is in some ways a greater determinant of later sexual violence than having been a victim yourself. What Ricky did was to try very hard to blame his sister for what was happening. That's what kids do. They have to live in the world. Mom's gone, Dad's doing this, and nobody is intervening. Social Services comes to the house fairly routinely, by the way, and they leave the children in the home over and over again; almost without exception, all my clients have thick Social Service files. These are not families, these are not children, who are unknown to us before they become the beasts that we don't want to know anymore. They are children who are in trouble and who we know are in trouble. In fact, one of the things that Ricky did was to take his little brother Doug out into the street, and because they had no food most of the time, they fed themselves from dumpsters from restaurants around their home town. Sometimes they stole food from convenience stores, and it was because of these convenience-store robberies that Social Services initially showed up in their home. There was one occasion when the mother came back for the children. The children got to see her beaten nearly to her death. Then she was carried off to the hospital, and they never saw her again.

One of the things that made Ricky crazy — and by the way, he doesn't fit any of the routine diagnoses; he might not even fit into the 50 percent of seriously mentally ill — one of the things that made him crazy was that he never got hit. While his sister was being brutalized and while his brother was being tied naked to an iron bed in the house and beaten bloody, nearly daily, Ricky never was touched. Apparently Dad thought Ricky was one of his special kids. And almost all the men I've worked with have been identified in their families as in some way unique or special. When the state's attorney asked me why it was this sibling and not the others, I told him what I'm telling you now: It's because siblings living in the same home are not all treated in the same way. They begin life as individuals. What's amazing to me is that more of these children don't grow up to be violent, not that some of them grow up to be violent people.

Okay, so now we've got Ricky about age twelve or thirteen. There's an incredible amount of pornography in his house. Most of my clients who've committed violent crimes associated with sex have been exposed to pornographic material in ways absolutely destructive to them. What happens in children is that they can not absorb, as we would absorb, and make discriminations about what they're viewing, and for Ricky women and violence were paired totally, forever, in a way that for him was impossible to separate. So what happens to a guy like this? Well, he starts to rape women. Are you surprised? I'm not surprised. And as he raped he became more and more angry with himself, more and angry about the world, and he ultimately committed a horrible murder. He murdered a sixteen-year-old girl. He was not caught for that murder. He was, in fact, in prison for another crime, when the man who'd been convicted of that murder became known to him. Ricky spent six months trying to convince the police in his county that he was, in fact, the murderer.

What we're talking about is extraordinary anger, extraordinary rage, extraordinary self-loathing. Anger at the world, anger at us, for not having protected him. Anger that comes out in very, very self-destructive ways, and ultimately in destructive ways against all of us.

I tell you all this because among my clients Ricky's life is not unique. One of the things that I have to do with myself is a mental gymnastics thing. I'm on an airplane with a file about a client, someone I've not met. I'm flying off to another state. Most of the time it's Florida or Texas, where they like the death penalty a lot, even more than we do here, and I'm reading about a crime. I'm reading about a monster who perpetrated a crime I cannot fathom. And I think to myself, how in the world am I going to sit in a room with this person for ten or twelve or twenty hours and then explain him to a jury, make him look and feel like a person? Well, guess what, y'all? He is a person, and as guilty as he is of the crime that brings him to trial for his life, or lands him on Death Row, what I meet is some boy like Ricky Sanderson.*

*Ricky Lee Sanderson was executed on January 29, 1998. One year later, columnist Susanna Rodell wrote in the *News & Observer*:

"Ricky could be alive today if he had exhausted all the appeals legally available to him. But in his newly awakened state he could not, he said, allow the family of the girl he had killed to go through the trauma of more court appearances, forced again to relive their nightmare. To accept his punishment was the least he could do for them. He could not bring their daughter back.

"When I met Ricky last year, a few days before his execution, I was not a

HENDERSON HILL
Attorney, Ferguson Stein Wallas Adkins Gresham & Sumter

Let me give you some numbers. On Death Row in North Carolina, as of the end of March: white males, 71; black males, 96; Indian males, 3; other males, 4; white females, 3. Total: 177. The next scheduled execution is a week from today — April 24; Wendell Flowers, African American, depressed and under medication.*

murderer. I was just a person, your normal mixture of motivations: Altruism and selfishness, anger and love. I was not, by normal definition, a criminal. But he had something I didn't have, and which I've come to identify as serenity.

"The first words I heard him speak, in the gray visitors room at Central Prison, were: There is no sorrow here.

"For the first time in his life, he told me, he had the certain feeling that he was acting on his conscience. That feeling was the greatest gift he could imagine, and the one thing no one could take from him....He was responsible for his crime; he would pay the penalty. He would not allow his lawyers to plead on his behalf. He asked only for the chance to speak, for as long as he was allowed to speak, of the miracle that had happened in his life. If God could change him, he reasoned, God could change anyone.

"....When he talked to me, his gaze was steady. I felt rattled and peaceful at the same time. Both feelings, I later concluded, came from the unfamiliar sensation of standing in such a place with my usual armor melting away, the journalist's cynicism in little puddles at my feet. Ricky looked at me and said he thought I was on the level. I thought he was too.

"In the days after they killed him, I walked around in some kind of shock. I kept seeing his big body, stilled, robbed of its complicated energy. Who had the right to do this, I wondered, to compound the original senseless crime with another? To make me and you, collectively, into murderers?

"Why am I bringing this up now? Because we live in cynical times. It's not fashionable to believe in renewal...I'm bringing it up to say, there was life here last year, that it's not here now, that it touched me, that I'm not the same person because of it.

"That a murderer gave me a gift that many righteous people could not give me, that I still don't entirely understand."

---

* Wendell Flowers was not executed as scheduled; he picked up his appeals and they are proceeding apace.

MARSHALL DYAN

Alcohol and drug use are frequently significant factors, not unrelated to problems of mental health. Lots of mentally ill people — when they don't get diagnosed and treated, they try to treat themselves by turning to alcohol and drugs.

FAYE SULTAN

Almost 90 percent of my clients began their substance abuse around or before the age of twelve. Early substance abusers medicate not for mental illness but to stand the pain of the environment they live in.

MARSHALL DYAN

It doesn't have to be hard drugs. Alcohol and marijuana are commonly the worst drugs involved. And alcohol is perceived by many as a drug that doesn't need a response.

FRANK BALLANCE

Of the 177 on Death Row, many committed their crimes before age eighteen. Those under seventeen cannot be executed. As for a mental health exemption, we don't have one in North Carolina. We tried to get the age exemption moved up to eighteen. We failed. We tried to legislate a mental health exemption. We failed.

MENTALLY RETARDED
AND JUVENILES

VERLA INSKO, MODERATOR
North Carolina State Representative, Twenty-fourth District

At the last session of the General Assembly we changed the family reunification law somewhat. We're not now required to send children back into domestic violence situations where they'll be further traumatized. There's been a shift in North Carolina from reunifying the family regardless, to having the judge being able at some point to say, "This is not a safe environment for this child and the child can be removed."

The Domestic Violence Study Commission, on which I serve, is studying the effects on children of observing domestic violence. Our Commission also is examining existing laws for possible revision. More personally, I'm involved in an effort to get another Whitaker School in the state, like the one currently operating in Butner. Whitaker School is a re-education center for teen-agers, ages fourteen to sixteen, who have severe behavioral problems. Most have had several contacts with the juvenile justice system and mental health services. As an approach to rehabilitating youth, re-education calls for an intense peer environment that, in addition to the regular school day, includes daily group meetings at which students confront their own dysfunctional behavior. They take responsibility for cooking, cleaning, and laundry, but the real work they do is to give up dysfunctional behavior and learn functional behavior. Over the first eighteen months after completing this program at the Butner center, 80 percent are still in school and performing successfully, and none has had any incidents with the law. This is a much higher success rate than we've had with any of our conventional training schools. Colorado and Arizona are using re-education in their juvenile treatment centers instead of the usual training-school approach, and I'd like to see more such centers here in North Carolina.

Another concern for me is to gain more mental health parity and to get more mental health services. People talk as if we do have mental health parity in insurance coverage, but we really don't. There are a lot of barriers to getting adequate mental health coverage.*

TOM LOFLIN
Criminal Defense Attorney; Partner, Loflin & Loflin

Thanks to the U.S. Supreme Court decision in *Thompson v. Oklahoma*, juveniles under the age of sixteen cannot now be sentenced to death anywhere in the United States.

The Supreme Court also ruled that it's perfectly fine to execute any person who is above the age of fifteen at the time he or she commits a capital crime.

As Frank Ballance implied, the North Carolina legislation that went into effect about a dozen or so years ago was a compromise. Frank's effort to eliminate the death penalty for minors was defeated. The General Assembly's response was, instead, to say, "Okay, we won't impose capital punishment on sixteen-year-olds. We will, however,

---

*In August 1998 mental-health advocates in North Carolina failed for the sixth time in as many years to get consideration by the General Assembly of a bill that would require employers who offer health insurance to provide equal coverage for mental disabilities and physical ailments (including parity on co-payments, deductibles, and lifetime dollar amounts). Opponents, led by the National Federation of Independent Business, have successfully argued that the bill as submitted would amount to a mandate on small businesses. To make the coverage optional, however, would "drive up the costs," according to the executive director of the N.C. Psychological Association, and probably make it prohibitively expensive. "Only those groups where somebody has a family member in need might be apt to take it."

impose it on seventeens, for seventeen is old enough." And that's the current state of law to do with juveniles convicted of capital crimes in North Carolina.

But thanks to special legislation, a couple of years ago, thirteen-year-olds now face life without parole in North Carolina. A thirteen-year-old juvenile who a district court judge finds probable cause to believe guilty of first-degree murder must be bound over to Superior Court for trial as an adult. If that juvenile is convicted of first-degree murder, he gets an adult sentence, which is life in prison, since he can't be given the death penalty. The only sentence for first-degree murder by a juvenile in North Carolina is life without parole. For all other felonies, including second-degree murder, the district court judge sitting in the juvenile court has the discretion to bind over the juvenile — a thirteen-year-old, a fourteen-year-old, or a fifteen-year-old — for trial as an adult. For at least the past thirty years, North Carolina has followed the rule that anyone sixteen or over is tried automatically in an adult court.

If you look at the current world view concerning juveniles — there's a convention called the UN Convention on the Rights of the Child. Only two countries have failed to ratify it, our country being one of them. Although it does not have a mechanism for enforcement, this convention does say that it is wrong, it is against international law, to execute a person if that person is under the age of eighteen, no matter what that person does. There's also an international convention on human rights. While the U.S. has signed this one, it has chosen to opt out on some key provisions. This convention also says that it is against international law to execute minors — that is, anybody under eighteen. You can guess one of the provisions that our country has declined to endorse. Apparently our country, which is supposed to be the premier country in the world, wants to be able to execute minors, even though almost all the other countries, including communist China, are signing compacts declaring it to be wrong. It's a disgrace.

[He holds up a ceramic sculpture of Dennis Rodman, the basketball player.] This was made by a fourteen-year-old boy from Liverpool, England, who at the age of eleven was tried as an adult for participating in a homicide when he was ten-and-a-half years old. It was a case that got some publicity in this country. It's usually described as the James Bulger case, because James Bulger was a two-year-old toddler who was abducted from a shopping center in Liverpool by two children not yet in their teens, taken to an abandoned railroad line and battered to death with bricks and an iron bar. This sculpture was made for my wife Ann by John Venables, one of the two children convicted.

This past March I had the privilege of helping argue John Venables' case before the European Commission on Human Rights in Strasbourg, France, which enforces the European Convention for Human Rights. This convention is enforceable because the European nations that signed it set up a court to do so and gave it the binding authority to interpret the laws of the convention for all signatory countries. We are making as one of our arguments that it is simply wrong under a provision similar to our Eighth Amendment — cruel and unusual punishment — to try a child at that age as an adult. I'm pleased to report that proceeding went very well. We may have actually established that principle in European law.

ANDREW SHORT
Psychologist, Charlotte

Some of you may be familiar with people with mental retardation. Mental retardation refers to persons with seriously impaired intellectual and adaptive capacities. A mentally retarded person is delayed in his ability to take care of himself or herself. Usually what we tell parents when we're working with them and diagnosing these problems in young children is that the children are showing delays and will continue to show delays as they grow older. They are behind their peers in their development, and they will continue to be behind throughout the spans of their lives. Most definitions of mental retardation include intellectual functioning, which refers to the capacity to learn, and to adaptive functioning, which refers to daily living skills and the ability to work. In some ways adaptive functioning is more critical, but both elements are necessary for a person to be considered retarded.

Some of the arguments about people with mental retardation and the death penalty tie in with some of the issues that have been raised already in terms of social class, because people with mental retardation tend to be poor. They don't tend to earn much money. Those that come from wealthy families — and they come from a range of families — are not the ones you'll find on Death Row.

Compared with so-called normal people, people with mental retardation lack judgment and understanding in the full range of situations they encounter. They are weak in the skills of communication, memory, and judgment. Generally, there's a neurological basis. They have deficits in impulsivity, in knowledge, and in moral development, as well as in areas of motivation and attention. In adulthood, all people who qualify as mentally retarded need some form of assistance to carry out their daily lives. They're often in some sort of sheltered living situation. In earlier years more were in institutions. Nowadays they're more likely to be in group homes, and sometimes in individual family situations, generally always in an arrangement that provides some kind and degree of assistance.

This became an issue when we tried unsuccessfully — we came up one vote short — to get some legislation through. The IQ cut-off almost universally used in the diagnostic systems is seventy, and we went to the legislature hoping to establish this as the standard in North

Carolina. What an IQ of seventy means specifically is that people with mental retardation are in the bottom 2 percent in terms of intellectual functioning and intellectual skills.

The American Association of Mental Deficiency's definition of mental retardation mirrors the one we used when we went to the General Assembly in 1993. The definition is basically three-pronged. In order to qualify as mentally retarded in one of these court cases, a person would have to show significantly subaverage intellectual functioning and deficits in adaptive functioning (there are tests in both these areas); an individual would have to score below seventy on both the intellectual measure and the adaptive functioning measure. We hear about people with low IQs who are able to perform at a high level in their daily lives; by our definition, which is strict, these people would not qualify as mentally retarded. And the final criterion — the third "prong" — is that the deficit must be manifested before the person is eighteen years old. This became important during the legislative effort because there was a lot of concern either that people would fake IQ tests or that the tests might somehow be skewed in order to get a person off on grounds of mental retardation. What we were able to come up with in the legislation is that almost everyone with subaverage intelligence will be identified as he or she goes through the state school system. This process creates a basic record of evidence that these persons have been qualified as being mentally retarded previous to any involvement in court proceedings. So we were able to use this to allay concern about the possible faking of IQ tests or the skewing of test results.

The common sense argument is that the death penalty as retribution is simply out of proportion to the personal blameworthiness of individuals with mental retardation. Moreover, because of their limited reasoning ability, their greater proclivity to impulsive acts, and their problems with such things as memory and attention and communication, it is unlikely that any of them will be deterred by the threat of a death penalty.

KEN ROSE
Director, Center for Death Penalty Litigation

I'm going to give just a brief outline of the decisional background by the U. S. Supreme Court on this issue. First, *Penry v. Lynaugh* 492 U.S. 302 in 1989, which challenged the constitutionality of the death penalty as it applied to persons with mental retardation. The argument in *Penry* was that in all cases where there is someone with mental retardation the death penalty is cruel and unusual punishment.

John Paul Penry had an IQ of fifty-four. He had the mental age of an eight-year-old. According to the briefs submitted, his ability to function in the world was that of a nine-or ten-year-old. The Supreme Court held that there was insufficient evidence of a national emerging consensus against execution of the mentally retarded, and consequently the Eighth Amendment was not violated by the killing of Mr. Penry.

At that time only two states — Georgia and Maryland — had enacted legislation exempting people with mental retardation from the death penalty. Since the *Penry* decision, they have been joined by several other states, among them New Mexico, Tennessee, Kentucky, Oregon, Washington, New York, Kansas, and Arkansas. But not by North Carolina. North Carolina has been conspicuously indifferent.

The polling data on this issue is instructive. Those of us who deal in death penalty cases are used to seeing statistics that show 80 percent of the population favoring the death penalty. But when asked if death should be imposed on the mentally retarded, between two-thirds and 80 percent of respondents say no. Even more noteworthy, a majority of those who support the death penalty oppose it for people with mental retardation. I do not have North Carolina data, but I would be surprised if on this issue the people of North Carolina differ much from the citizens of Louisiana or Georgia, or that the results of a state poll would depart significantly from those in the most recent national poll, which shows 70 percent opposed.

The American Association on Mental Retardation has not taken a position on the death penalty. It has, however, vigorously opposed its imposition on any individual mentally retarded. So have the National Association for Retarded Citizens, the American Psychological Association, the Association for Persons with Severe Handicap, the American Association of University Affiliated Programs for the Developmentally Disabled, and numerous other organizations. These professional and voluntary organizations represent the broadest possible spectrum of viewpoints within the field.

Now, why should all persons with mental retardation be excluded from the death penalty? There's a strong argument, I think, that persons with severe mental illness should also be excluded, and I tend to agree. But why should everyone within the group of persons with mental retardation be excluded? Let me read some of the reasons given by Jim Ellis, a former president of the American Association on Mental Retardation:

"It is important to remember that... only about 1 or 2 percent of all persons convicted of murder in this country are sentenced to death. We reserve the death penalty for those persons who have supposedly committed the worst of crimes, or who have had the most terrible backgrounds, and we don't give the death penalty to the average person who commits murder." (In North Carolina it's about 2 to 3 percent of all murderers.) According to Dr. Ellis, in case after case the Supreme Court has made personal culpability and moral blameworthiness the determining criteria for selecting the one in a hundred who may be sentenced to death. Personal culpability and moral blameworthiness. That's all.

Now, a key element in establishing moral culpability is the defendant's state of mind and his level of understanding of his unlawful act. To permit the execution of a person with mental retardation requires that such an individual be simultaneously in the top 1 percent of the population in his understanding of the wrongfulness of his action, and in the bottom 2 or 3 percent of the population in intelligence. As a practical matter, no one can be in both categories, so if we reserve the death penalty for the persons who are most morally blameworthy, we cannot give it to persons with mental retardation.

There is another very, very significant reason that we should exclude persons with mental retardation. It may be more important than any of the others. In cases where our clients have limited intelligence, there is a higher risk of mistaken conviction, of mistaken confession, or of erroneous information. Persons with mental retardation often have an inordinate desire to please authority figures. That can lead to false confessions. Several examples of such flawed interrogations and false confessions are cited in Robert Perske's Unequal Justice, one of them about a young man in Missouri with organic brain damage named Johnny Lee Wilson. In the confession introduced as evidence, the detective asked Wilson, "What else was around the victim's ankle?"

Wilson said, "I'm thinking."

Detective: "What are some of the things that could be used?"

Wilson: "Handcuffs, I think."

Detective: "No, no, wrong answer."

After Johnny Lee Wilson's conviction, evidence turned up that another person may have committed the crime.

One more example: David Vasquez, Virginia.

Detective: "Okay, tell us how it went, David. Tell us how you did it."

Vasquez: "She told me to grab a knife and stab her. That's all."

Detective: "No, David."

Vasquez: "If it did happen and I did it, and my fingerprints were on it."

Detective, yelling. "You hung her."

Vasquez: "What?"

Detective, shouting: "You hung her."

Vasquez: "Okay, So I hung her."

David Vasquez pleaded guilty and received forty years for second-degree murder and fifteen years for burglary. Subsequent investigation found the real murderer. After five years, Vasquez was pardoned by the governor of Virginia.

Another problem: Many defendants are ashamed of being mentally retarded and will try to hide it. It's something they may not feel good about, or sense that it's something bad about themselves. They may have been told throughout their lives, "It's bad to be mentally retarded." They have been called names by their peers. So, naturally, they try to mask their condition. Several of my cases have gone through trial with no determination and no investigation on mental retardation. I've learned that my client is mentally retarded only when I see the post-conviction record. So it's an important issue. If we enacted legislation that exempted persons with mental retardation from the death penalty, my guess is that every attorney would feel it necessary to check into the mental competence and adaptive skills of his client.

Here's something else from Jim Ellis: "Centuries ago Sir Edward Coke explained the law's prohibition on executing an insane person by describing it as a miserable spectacle...of extreme inhumanity and cruelty and can be no example to others." In modern times the execution of a person with mental retardation matches that description. Any imposition of the death penalty unsupported by a valid public purpose is "nothing more than a purposeless and needless imposition of pain and suffering." And that is what I suggest we are doing in this society now when we sentence to death someone with mental retardation.

ADAM STEIN
Former Appellate Defender for the State

I've represented four children on appeal from death sentences. The first occasion came in 1967 when Julius Chambers called me to his office and said, "This is a criminal appeal that we just got, and you've got to do it." And he handed me this little file on sixteen-year-old Marie Hill from Rocky Mount.

We're talking some today about the problems of counsel in capital cases. Here I was, a kid just out of law school who wasn't even a member of the North Carolina bar yet, doing a brief for Marie Hill who had been sentenced to death. But in one way my inexperience did not matter. Her trial lawyer in Rocky Mount had gotten her through the whole superior court system in about a day and a half, including jury selection, so there wasn't a daunting, massive record for a young lawyer, as is so often true in capital cases.

My next appeal, a couple of years later, was a fifteen-year-old boy, Robert Louis Roseboro, who'd been convicted of murder in Shelby. He was said to have killed a woman who ran a little outlet store. The evidence was circumstantial. The boy was obviously very troubled. He may well have done it.

Both these cases were under the prior regime, when at the end of a trial a jury pronounced its verdict on guilt and punishment at the same time. The verdict might be guilty with a death penalty without the jury's hearing any evidence or the lawyer's giving any attention to the appropriate punishment. One might think that the obvious fact that these two defendants were children would have tipped the scales against death, but it did not.

My next appeal, also under the old system, was from Orange County. Johnny Lee Edwards was sixteen. He was convicted of going into a woman's house just outside Carrboro and killing her. He was sentenced to die. And, more recently, under the new statute, I handled the appeal for Leon Brown from Red Springs, who had allegedly participated in a crime where the evidence showed three other young men to have been involved, one of them his brother. Leon was by far the youngest. With his brother, he was convicted of the very grisly rape-murder of a twelve-year-old neighbor girl.

I would be preaching to the choir if I suggested to this audience that there's something wrong about holding fully blameworthy children fifteen years and sixteen years old. But besides the common denominator of youth, these cases had in them a number of the other factors that the ABA noted in its call for a moratorium. Marie Hill, who came from the wrong side of the tracks in Rocky Mount, went to a neighborhood store after school and bludgeoned the shopkeeper. Her case got routine handling in the criminal justice system as if the crime were not very serious. Certainly the factors of race, class, age in her case, contributed to the death verdict; we do not know whether there was also mental retardation, or a history of abuse. Nobody cared to look.

Robert Louis Roseboro was not only young; he also was poor and black. So was Johnny Lee Edwards. Now, the interesting thing about Johnny Lee's case was how he was represented by his trial lawyer. He was arrested late at night. The sheriff called one of the district court judges and said, "We've arrested this boy. He says he murdered Mrs. Cole [the mother of a Chapel Hill lawyer]." So the judge said, "Call soandso" — naming a lawyer now deceased — "in Hillsborough. Have him go over there to represent him." Well, the lawyer from Hillsborough went over there. He didn't meet with his client separately. Instead, he asked the sheriff, "What's going on?" and the sheriff said,

"He said he killed the lady." And the sheriff turned to the boy and said, "Go on, son, tell the lawyer what happened." So Johnny Lee Edwards gave a confession to his lawyer in front of the sheriff. Now, the North Carolina Supreme Court said the second confession was the fruit of the first confession and the first confession was bad because Johnny Lee was a juvenile. (As I remember, the statute back then said a juvenile had the right to have a parent, or an adult, present when questioned by the police.) Well, the case came back, the court appointed the same lawyer to represent him for trial, and Johnny Lee got convicted again. I was the volunteer lawyer for the second appeal. I followed the script from my first and got my client a third trial.

I wasn't asked to do the appeal on the third trial, and Johnny Lee was convicted on the evidence of a jail-house confession. They'd decided that all these confessions obtained from the sheriff weren't going to work, so they'd brought in a woman inmate who was being detained in the jail who said that Johnny Lee had told her he'd done it, and she recounted the confession he gave. Now, anybody who practiced law in Orange County knew that the women's cell in the old jail, where she was, was so removed from where Johnny Lee was that the two could not have talked to each other. It was physically impossible. But Johnny Lee's lawyer, who practiced in Hillsborough, didn't challenge this aspect of the confession at all. As a consequence, the conviction was affirmed, this time with a life sentence. Johnny Lee served his time, and he probably got out. Goodness knows what has happened to him since.

As with Johnny Lee Edwards, there was clear neglect by counsel in the Marie Hill case. People got more attention and better defenses for drunk driving. As for Leon Brown, he could have been a poster child for the moratorium. He was not only fifteen and black, he was also very much a secondary actor, a sort of tagalong. He was also mentally retarded, though it barely shows in the record. After the appeal, I worked on the retrial, which was separated from his brother's, and Dr. George Baroff, who's done wonderful work with mental retardation, assisted us. We challenged Leon's confession for all the reasons that Ken Rose enumerated. Well, the Supreme Court didn't throw the confession out but, at the end of the state's case the murder charge was dismissed. Leon ended up getting a life sentence. At the first trial, the lawyer had mounted almost no defense.

This case is also an example of a significant disability for a person with mental retardation. Leon had a second-degree murder plea offer during the trial that would have allowed him to be released for time served. He turned it down. He was intellectually unable to deal with the abstract notion of accepting a plea bargain to get the best bargain. He couldn't do that. What he could do was figure out that it made him feel better to say he was not guilty, and that was the way we went. It was pretty frustrating for a defense lawyer.

I don't think there are many people in this room who think we can really clean all this up. But it certainly could be better, and we should make some real effort to make it better. Having the kind of representation that Marie Hill and Johnny Lee Edwards and Leon Brown had in their first trials — it's a joke to suggest that we're providing any measure of justice.

But we should also understand that children can still be convicted, even when they're represented by wonderful lawyers. There was a mention of Roger and Wade Smith representing this wealthy person. Well, it's very important — if you're charged with murder — to have Wade and Roger represent you. They're great, caring lawyers, and that often makes a difference. But sometimes what is more important is who you are; status can figure very heavily. Roger had a case not long ago in which his client was a migrant Mexican worker and Roger's client got the death penalty despite powerful mitigating evidence. To the list of defendants who got the death penalty despite excellent representation, I add Robert Louis Roseboro, the fifteen-year-old I mentioned earlier. He was represented by my partners, Julius Chambers and James Ferguson — in my view, a dream team. But that jury in Shelby could not be moved.

The death penalty remains arbitrary. On factors that people universally recognize as having strong mitigating value, this jury can say yes, this jury can say no. At best — and it seldom is "at best" — it's a crap shoot.

What the Constitution Says and Doesn't Say

James Exum, Jr.
Former Chief Justice of the North Carolina Supreme Court

Fundamentally, almost intuitively, I have always thought the death penalty, far from reducing violence, actually promotes it.

Twenty-eight years ago, in 1975, shortly after I got on the court, I had to face the case on which I was going to make a difference; at least I was going to have a vote on the question of the constitutionality of the death penalty in North Carolina at that time. I hadn't revisited this opinion in many, many years. I did so in preparation for my appearance with you today, and what I said in my opinion was this: "Whether the death penalty is constitutional is not an easy question for me, for I am personally opposed to capital punishment. Maintaining it even for murder is not, in my view, wise public policy."

I went on to say: "My belief that capital punishment is not wise public policy is based on the proposition that government if it functions properly should seek to set an example, to teach the people whom it serves. People ought to be able to look at the basic underlying policies of government and see there what is inherently right and proper." I quoted this great statement from Justice Brandeis: "Our government is the potent omnipresent teacher. For good or for ill, it teaches the whole people by its example.'" Then I wrote, "The cold calculated premeditated taking of human life is an act the brutality and violence of which is not diminished because it is sponsored by the state. We abhor the kind of human beings who commit such an act. That the state should respond in kind is equally abhorrent. The argument that we somehow exalt human life by executing those who murder falls of its own weight. Calculated killings by individuals without doubt cheapen the God-given right to live. So, however, do calculated executions at the hand of the state. Executions are bad examples. They teach not respect for life but that some lives are not worth maintaining. It is a short step in the minds of many from execution at the hands of the state to murder and other violence at the hands of the people."

It's amazing how my views have remained relatively stable over twenty-eight years. Even if wrong, I've at least been consistent in that position: The death penalty actually promotes violence in our society rather than diminishes it.

As a legislator in 1967, I voted to abolish the death penalty as a matter of public policy. My views were known when I campaigned in Guilford County. I got elected despite that. In those days, there was a bill offered almost every session of the General Assembly to abolish the death penalty. And we had a substantial minority willing to abolish it. The votes were very close in those days.

Over my life I guess I've had as much an opportunity to consider the efficacy of the death penalty as anybody in the room, probably more. And I've become convinced that if we're going to win this battle, and get the death penalty abolished as an instrument of criminal justice, it's not going to be in our courts. It's not going to be through the law. It's got to be done politically. Almost all the arguments we're hearing today are really public policy arguments. They're public policy reasons. And there are others we haven't heard. For instance — and this is a point not often made — proponents of the death penalty often talk as if sentencing is a matter of death or nothing; if we don't sentence convicted murderers to death, they say, we're not going to punish them. That's not the dynamic. The right question is, will it be death or life imprisonment without possibility of parole? And the issue is, is all the trouble and all the expense, all the polarization that it creates — not only in society but in our legal profession as well — is all of this worth whatever difference there might be between punishment by death on the one hand and life imprisonment without parole on the other? Public policy-wise, the answer to me is clearly no.

I have never gotten much help from our Constitution on this issue. I've never been able to construct in my own mind a constitutional argument against the death penalty. Indeed, in North Carolina the Constitution explicitly provides for death as a punishment. So it's rather hard to say that death is unconstitutional when the Constitution says we've got it.

I've had a couple of opportunities to exchange views with Chief Justice Rehnquist. Like me, he has a hard time saying there's anything unconstitutional about the death penalty. When I told him what our North Carolina constitution provided, he said, "We've got the same problem with the federal government." And I said, "Well, I didn't know the federal constitution said anything about death." He said it did, and he's got a point: The Fifth and the Fourteenth amendments do say that we won't deprive anybody of life without due process of law. The implication is that if you accord due process of law, you can deprive somebody of his life.

My point is, judges have a very hard time constructing arguments to abolish the death penalty under the constitutions of our nation and state as they now exist. Very plainly, the battle is going to have to be fought on public policy grounds on the political front.

Chief Justice Warren's opinion in the 1958 case, *Trop v. Dulles*, is eminently relevant: "The Eighth Amendment must draw its meaning from the evolving standards of decency that mark the progress of a maturing society." You know why the Court held that the punishment in *Trop v. Dulles* violated the cruel-and-unusual provision of the Eighth Amendment? It was because it didn't meet the evolving standards of a maturing society in 1958. You remember what the punishment was? The defendant in that case had been convicted of desertion. He was a military man who had been court- martialed for desertion in time of war. The statute said that anyone convicted of this crime would be deprived of citizenship. But a majority of the U. S. Supreme Court said that this punishment — depriving someone of citizenship — was cruel and unusual. The court said, "There may be involved no physical mistreatment, no primitive torture. There is instead the total destruction of the individual's status in organized society. It is a form of punishment more primitive than torture, for it destroys for the individual the political existence that was centuries in developing. The punishment strips the citizen of his status in the national and international political community."

When I read those words, I said, "Well, my goodness, if the taking of somebody's status as a citizen in the national and international community violates the cruel-and-unusual clause of the Eighth Amendment, why doesn't taking his life?." I don't know. Is *Trop v. Dulles* still good law, or has it been overruled? Although it's still on the books, later decisions have made it relatively clear that taking life is not a violation of the Eighth Amendment, provided due process is accorded.

For many years on the Court, I had hoped we could make some sense out of the death penalty. Given the new statutes, which set up a lot of hoops through which the prosecution has to jump, and given proportionality review, which entitles the Court to look at a case to see indeed whether there is any evidence of capriciousness or discrimination, I had hoped we could sensibly reserve the death penalty — if we have to have it — for those cases that are the most heinous, the most awful. Toward the end of my career on the Court, I gave up on the idea of ever being able to do that with any rationality. I just came to the conclusion that the law was never going to let us do that. I decided, as Professor Charles Black put it many, many years ago, that "while the justice of God may be sufficient, the justice of man will forever be incapable of deciding rationally who should live and who should die."

But that idea doesn't translate very easily into constitutional doctrine because judges don't ordinarily look at the landscape when they decide a case. They look at the individual case. They look at this individual defendant, and they try to decide whether something was awry in this case that makes the death penalty unconstitutional or inappropriate.

So the battleground of the death penalty does not lie with the judiciary. It does not lie with our courts. It lies in the political arena with our legislators.

My hope personally lies with future generations. I believe that we are more humane than our fathers and grandfathers. I believe our children and grandchildren will probably be more humane than we. It's not easy to see it sometime, but I think over the sweep of history this is true. Our hope in this arena, as in others, lies with future generations.

PANEL III
RACE AND CLASS
MICKEY MICHAUX, MODERATOR,
23rd District Representative to the General Assembly

You may remember that the death sentence in North Carolina used to be inflicted against those who'd committed first-degree murder, first-degree arson, first-degree burglary, and first-degree rape. But after the decision in the *Furman* case came down, the General Assembly moved to re-examine every aspect of the state law.

During the 1975 session we were able to cut off the death penalty for first-degree burglary, first-degree arson, and rape. We failed, however, to abolish it for first-degree murder.

For those of us in the Legislature opposed to capital punishment, the decisions we had to make were heart-rending. What were we going to do? We had three bills — one that permitted the death penalty only in case of first-degree murder; another that gave it in first-degree murder and rape; and a third that kept the status quo. I didn't want to vote for any of them. Nevertheless, something had to be done. A decision had to be made.

In the House we had worked the bills around to the point where the death-penalty bill against first-degree murder was first on the calendar. The other two followed. Well, one of the things politicians sometimes learn to do is to count heads, count numbers, and when we looked around the General Assembly as it was composed at that time, there was the awful possibility that the death penalty would go back to its original status, of its being imposed on all four categories. So, many of us who were adamantly opposed to the death penalty were put in the position where we had to choose the least of three evils. That's why we'd gotten that bill put on first, where the death penalty would be limited to first-degree murder. And let me tell you, that bill passed the House by a very, very, very slim majority.

JACK BOGER
Professor and Associate Dean of Academic Affairs
UNC-CH School of Law

In 1978, by blind luck, I found myself at the NAACP Legal Defense Fund. For forty years prior to that time, Thurgood Marshall, Jack Greenberg, and others at LDF had frequently represented black defendants, typically in the South, typically charged with rape or murder against white victims. They became involved in these cases because of the procedural travesties that often accompanied the trials, but they noticed larger patterns — indeed, no one could help but notice larger patterns in the imposition of sentences in the South and elsewhere in the country. These patterns demonstrated that black defendants were far more often sent to death for the same crimes than were their white co-defendants. And indeed — and this was a more subtle point — that when white persons were the victims of the crime, it was far more likely that death would be imposed no matter what race the defendant. Several early studies in the 1940s emanating from the University of North Carolina — by Guy Mangum, Guy Johnson, and Harold Garfinkel — noted that pattern in North and South Carolina and Georgia capital cases. But there seemed very little to do about it except to continue to defend criminal cases on constitutional grounds, until the early 1960s. At that time Justice Arthur Goldberg, sitting on the Supreme Court, in effect invited lawyers throughout the country to come forward with a suggestion that imposition of the death penalty might be unconstitutional because of racial discrimination. Picking up that invitation, the Legal Defense Fund and the American Civil Liberties Union decided to try to show systematically that race was playing an impermissible part in death sentencing around the country.

Now the gross figures were extraordinary. If you look at who had been executed from 1930 to 1960 — let me read you the numbers: Of 3,984 lawfully executed, 2,113 were black — more than 50 percent; yet blacks constituted only 12, 14, at most 15 percent of the population. If you look at the crime of rape, the numbers were even more dramatic. From 1930 to 1965, 453 men were executed for rape. Of these, 407 were black. These data created a powerful, intuitive case that there was a racial bias. Yet they were nowhere good enough to satisfy the scrupulous demands of the law. To defend their death-sentencing patterns, state attorneys general would maintain, "There are explanations for these apparent disparities. The explanations are that in fact black crime is different; it's more aggravated, the offenders have longer prior records, it's not really race at all." To counter this kind of claim, what was needed was exhausting social scientific evidence on the characteristics of each case. What one had to do was to go out and look at a thousand cases and catalog all the relevant factors about each: The number of prior felonies the defendants had been convicted of, whether there was a contemporary felony at the time of the murder, whether there were multiple victims, whether the victims were young and defenseless, whether the crime was among acquaintances or among strangers. There are hundreds of factors that plausibly explain outcomes in capital cases. Once all that information has been collated and cataloged in social scientific form, then you are ready to ask, "If we hold all factors constant, if we look at the same kind of cases — if we have a thousand convenience- store homicides, 500 by black defendants and 500 by whites, and if all defendants have the same prior record, and if all involve a single gunshot wound during the course of a felony, *do the same percentage of defendants receive death sentences irrespective of their race and the race of their victims?* If one could show that 80 percent of the black defendants were getting death while only 50 percent of the white defendants were getting death, then one would be able to say, "We held constant all the factors that matter, and race continues to play a part."

So that was the challenge from the 1960s to the middle 1980s, to get that data. It was very hard to get. Think about North Carolina. There are a hundred counties. The trial records are in a hundred courthouses. Indeed, if the cases didn't go to trial, if a defendant accepted a prosecutor's offer to plead guilty to some lesser offense, then there'd be no trial record at all, except in the prosecutor and police files, which are not open. The Legal Defense Fund and its social scientific allies twice — once in the 1960s and once in the early 1980s — went to gather that kind of data. In the '80s, they found in Georgia that, even when all the other relevant factors were held constant, if the race of the victim was white it was 4.3 times more likely that death would be imposed.

With these data, LDF went to the federal courts to insist that this violated the equal-protection clause of the Fourteenth Amendment and that it was arbitrary and capricious under the cruel-and-unusual-punishment clause of the Eighth Amendment. The claim went to the Supreme Court of the United States and in 1987, by a five-to-four vote, the Court disagreed. The opinion was written by Justice Lewis Powell. Some years later, after he had retired from the Court, Justice Powell told a biographer, "This was the one decision that I rendered that I regret."

His decision largely foreclosed federal constitutional challenge in the courts to racial discrimination. Yet the social science data continues to mount that these racial patterns persist.

BARRY NAKELL

Former Professor, UNC-CH School of Law

The McCleskey case (*McCleskey v. Kemp*, 1987) is, I believe, the only case in which the U. S. Supreme Court has said expressly that racial discrimination does not invalidate a governmental program; that racial discrimination in the death penalty, as well as arbitrariness in the death penalty, is okay. In my judgment, the Supreme Court thereby overturned the 1972 landmark decision in *Furman v. Georgia*, in which it essentially held that the death penalty was being applied in such arbitrary fashion that it was unconstitutional, that there was no way to distinguish between cases that got the death penalty and cases that did not, that getting the death penalty was like being hit by lightning. It was that arbitrary.

North Carolina and other states responded by trying to develop systems that would guide or structure the capital decision-making process. In 1976, the Supreme Court upheld these systems, ruling that they appeared capable of controlling the exercise of discretion in the capital sentencing process. At the same time, the Court struck down that part of the North Carolina response that attempted to impose a mandatory capital sentencing system. North Carolina then adopted the guidelines approved by the Court.

I then undertook to find out whether the new procedures put in effect were, in fact, capable of controlling the exercise of discretion in the capital decision-making process in such a way as to avoid the arbitrariness that the Supreme Court had struck down in Furman. I began using a method that Professor Pollitt and I had tried a few years before but had to abandon because of our inability to get the needed data.

By this time North Carolina had developed a uniform medical examiner system. All homicides now had to go through the medical examiner, Page Hudson, who agreeably cooperated in our study. With his help we were able to get data on every homicide in the state, which enabled us to follow every homicide through the criminal justice process until it got diverted off the track of prosecution. We studied every homicide case that arose in North Carolina under the first year of the homicide statute. We studied each case through every discrete stage of the criminal process, using data from the medical examiner's office. We used information in the files of the prosecution and defense attorneys, we interviewed the prosecuting and defense attorneys, and we assembled and studied all the court records, thanks to a grant from the National Science Foundation. We followed a statistical method called Logistic Regression Analysis. I didn't, and don't, understand this method, but we had a couple of very fine statisticians from the university who did. And the results showed that there were both arbitrariness and discrimination in the imposition of the death penalty in North Carolina during the study year. We defined arbitrariness simply as being the imposition of the death penalty without regard to the legal standards. We took the legal standards for capital murder or first-degree murder, and the legal standard for aggravating and mitigating circumstances, and we developed a mathematical way of evaluating these. The first question we asked was whether the legal factors determined the outcome, and in a great number of cases the answer was yes, the legal factors were pretty determinant. But remember, we were studying a class of cases, all of them homicides to begin with, and all the defendants were subject to some penalty. So we didn't expect a total divergence from legal standards.

But we found a substantial amount of decision-making that could not be explained by the legal factors. This led us to examine divergence by using some nonlegal criteria, particularly racial or gender factors. And we found substantial divergence on both grounds, particularly racial. Our primary finding, however, was that whether a particular case had sufficient basis to be prosecuted as a capital case depended on the judicial district in which it was brought. We found extremely wide divergence among the policies of different prosecutors throughout the state, enough to give almost capricious meaning to the death penalty in practice. The most arbitrariness, as well as discrimination, in death-sentence processing occurred in those stages under the control of the prosecutor — primarily on decisions to go forward with a case as a capital case, but also on decisions to plea bargain. The North Carolina Supreme Court did eventually say that if there are capital factors in the case, the prosecutor is obligated to prosecute it as a capital case. In our study year that was not happening. There were many, many cases that were similar, if not identical, even within judicial districts, where prosecutors diverted some from the death penalty track by engaging in plea bargaining and took others to capital trial. We also found that when a case got to trial, the jury was more fair than the judges. It was at this point that the race of the victim appeared most significant; there was substantial discrimination in decisions to impose the death penalty, based on the race of the victim as well as on the race of the defendant.

This disparity in the imposition of the death penalty is something that in the *McCleskey* case the Supreme Court case said was not of constitutional significance. Justice Brennan wrote a dissenting opinion, saying that the pattern of arbitrariness in imposition of the death penalty violates the standards set in *Furman*, and Justice Marshall wrote another dissenting opinion saying that discrimination on the basis of race renders a death sentence unconstitutional.

In all these cases, the defendants arguably could have qualified for the death penalty. We took a pool of cases where presumably under the law there were enough factors to justify the death penalty. In some of these cases, defendants were sentenced to death; in others, defendants were not, regardless of what the legal standards would call for. Does this matter? Well, one argument made is that this is the way the criminal justice system works; there is unfairness throughout. True, as well established by both field and statistical evidence. The question is, whether the death penalty *is* different. The

Supreme Court has said in some cases that death is different. In some cases it has said that procedures necessary and acceptable in the imposition of criminal justice generally are simply unacceptable when we impose the ultimate penalty of death. But here in *McCleskey* the Supreme Court disregarded the principle that the death penalty is different and more demanding and more rigorous with regard to procedural due process. It said instead that we can accept a measure of arbitrariness and a measure of discrimination acceptable in no other area where it has been so substantially established. I think that certainly the injustice of an unjust dispensation of mercy is different from the injustice of an unjust execution. *Furman*, however, held that at some point disparity becomes systemic, not merely incidental, and the divergent decisions that effectively modify the law in practice for some defendants while others remain subject to the law as written, impose this kind of arbitrariness. The law before *McCleskey*, I believe, was certainly trending toward making this kind of arbitrariness, as well as discrimination, grounds for rendering death-penalty sentencing unconstitutional. In *McCleskey*, the Supreme Court simply chose, by a very narrow majority, to reverse that trend.

SKIP ALSTON
President, NC State Conference of NAACP Branches

African Americans have been looking at the death penalty for a number of years. We look at it as a legalized way of killing African Americans. More whites than African Americans commit serious crimes. But most whites do not receive the death penalty. Why? Because they have better representation; they have a better chance in the courts.

The NAACP is addressing this disparity on a daily basis across the country. Here in North Carolina we're monitoring the cases now of African Americans on Death Row, trying to determine whether or not they have gotten fair treatment in the courts. We are also trying to provide representation for those who cannot afford the Johnny Cochrans of the world. We're insisting on fair representation from our courts, from our lawyers, from our public defenders, and from our judges.

JACK BOGER

We've had twenty-six years now since *Furman*. The burden of proof ought to shift to those who think capital punishment is needed, is useful. Has it really been? Are we really more safe, more just? Have we had a decrease in the rate of criminal homicide that's not tied to the demographics of the population? I think the burden of proof ought to mean, we go to the General Assembly and say, "Have a moratorium and look at your own ambivalence."

VOICE FROM AUDIENCE

I think the current practice — middle of the night executions — is not accidental. It reflects the moral ambivalence that the country feels about capital punishment. Executions couldn't stand the full light of day in public. Maybe we ought to go back to the day when we had public executions.

BARRY NAKELL

Another factor that shows the ambivalence: We passed the death-penalty statute in 1976, and here twenty-two years later we can count on the fingers of both hands the total number of people who've been executed in that time. Jim Exum and Harry Martin know very well the workload this has imposed on the courts. I think the North Carolina Supreme Court must spend 50 percent of its time on capital cases.

JAMES EXUM

Seventy percent.

VOICE

About this proposition that a return to public executions would generate more opposition to the death penalty. I'd like to ask our psychologists here. What evidence do you have that public executions would help our cause, help us get this issue resolved? I have an idea that many people, more than we care to think, might even enjoy public executions, about the same way they enjoy dog fights.

VOICE FROM AUDIENCE

In the nineteenth century public executions were commonplace. Did the pattern change because the general public developed different laws, different standards of decency, more sensitivity to overt and cruel forms of punishment?

MICHAEL HAMDEN
From audience

If we had public executions today? Anybody who's been associated with a capital crime knows full well that by the time the prosecutor got through whipping people into a mob, stirring their base emotions, people would rush convicted murderers out to the town square and hang them. That's what would happen. We'd have public executions even in Chapel Hill if they could get it through the Legislature.

MICKEY MICHAUX

Let me pose a question to the panel. Is the death penalty a failure? Barry?

BARRY NAKELL

All the evidence shows the death penalty to be no deterrent. Of course, the argument is made that it deters the one person who's executed, but that kind of deterrence could be effected by incarceration. People talk about the death penalty being less expensive. All the evidence shows that a system with the death penalty is much more expensive than a system without it. How costly must it be, that our Supreme Court spends 70 percent of its time on capital cases! There are urgent motions on the eve of an execution. We had one case where our attorney general had three lawyers in Washington, a lawyer in Richmond at the Fourth Circuit, and a couple of lawyers in Raleigh at the North Carolina Supreme Court, to try to get a man executed that night. A justice of the United States Supreme Court denied the stay, and then Judge Phillips of the Fourth Circuit granted the stay, and then the whole Supreme Court had to sit in the wee hours of the morning trying to decide whether they could reverse the stay. This was not to decide whether to kill this man, but whether to kill him that night. All that effort.

A Death Row is tremendously difficult to maintain. It's much more expensive than it is to maintain a general prison population, and it causes many more problems for the prison system. Trials are much more expensive because every capital question goes to trial. You can't plead guilty to first-degree murder and the death penalty; you have to have a trial. Almost all cases have two trials. Many are retried, over and over again. There are more experts in capital cases, and double the number of lawyers. The costs of a system with capital punishment are enormous compared with those to support a system without it.

The death penalty does no discernible good in preventing homicide. And as all the social science data prove, there is an appalling, unconscionable amount of arbitrariness and discrimination in the way it's carried out.

All this is known. It's not a matter of opinion or conjecture. It's demonstrably true, verified by virtually every research method known to the social sciences. Yet it's all ignored. Is the death penalty a failure? Of course it is. And yet we continue to have a death penalty on the books in North Carolina. Why?

Skip Alston

Any time an innocent man, an innocent woman, is put to death, that's something you can't correct. It's happened, it happens, and it will happen again. A person will be put to death and all of a sudden we find out, too late, that he or she was innocent and should have been freed. How can we correct a wrong like that? We can't.

PANEL IV
INADEQUACY OF COUNSEL AND LEGAL PROCESS

ELLIE KINNAIRD, MODERATOR
N.C. Senator, Sixteenth District

I come from Minnesota, which has no death penalty. It never occurred to us in Minnesota that death was a proper outcome of criminal procedure, so I have been conditioned to take an active role in protesting the death penalty.

This is not, believe me, a stand that plays well in some parts of my district. To be opposed to capital punishment in North Carolina — that's tough for any politician. No doubt about it. You always have to be thinking that there are people who will not understand and who will penalize you.

Probably the toughest vote I've ever had to cast came on the bill to allow the families of victims to attend executions. I voted against that bill, along with Frank Ballance. The TV people thought my position was pretty interesting, so I was interviewed a couple of times. The interviews didn't win me any votes, but I welcomed the opportunity to make a statement about an issue I feel strongly about — a moral issue that people should be concerned about.

TYE HUNTER
Appellate Defender for the State of North Carolina

One time there was a pretty high profile case to be argued in the state Supreme Court. Lacy Thornburg was then the attorney general and I guess he'd been teased by some of his predecessors that he'd never actually gone up and argued a case. And so Attorney General

Thornburg, now Judge Thornburg, came up and delivered what I guess you'd call a little five-minute speech, and then graciously told the court that his assistant would handle any questions. In our little shop, we've always wondered if we could invoke the Thornburg rule and refer questions to someone else if the court was inclined to ask questions. But we're not going to invoke the Thornburg rule this afternoon, so —

LOU BILIONIS
Professor, UNC-CH School of Law

Many of you may recall Thurgood Marshall's impassioned dissents to the Supreme Court's affirmation of capital punishment in the 1970s. In those dissents, Justice Marshall argued that an informed citizenry would take a dimmer view of the death penalty than the uninformed citizenry that makes up much of popular opinion in America and to whom judges and legislators frequently react. His argument comes back to my mind today because in many ways this group is doing just the kind of important work that Marshall hoped would be undertaken — educating the citizenry to the realities of the death penalty.

The ABA similarly proceeds in the spirit of Justice Marshall, as evidenced by the fact that it is the ABA's call for a moratorium that brings us here. It may be well for us to ponder how remarkable this happens to be. We are not talking about dyed-in-the-wool abolitionists calling for a moratorium on capital punishment. We are talking about the largest organization of lawyers in America, many of whom had no problem with capital punishment whatsoever until they were asked to confront the facts brought to light by the resolution, and many of whom want the death penalty to remain a fixture in the criminal justice system. What should we make of this? What it says to me is that even in a nation that wants the death penalty, this death penalty — the one we have now — is unacceptable. Given the principles held fundamental in our nation — principles to which proponents and opponents of capital punishment alike subscribe — the present death penalty system will not do. It is indecent. It must change.

This afternoon we are asked to address one dimension of this — the problem of counsel and the adequacy of legal services provided to capital defendants. Let me try to frame what I understand the ABA's position to be on the matter, drawing for background on what Barry Nakell developed a short while ago in his discussion of arbitrariness.

No one thinks that individuals should live or die by the luck of the draw. No decent person thinks that some criminal defendants should live and some should die because the former have better lawyers than the latter. No one suggests that we should hand out demerits to a capital defendant on the ground that a poor lawyer makes him more eligible for the death penalty, or that bonus points should be awarded a capital defendant on the ground that a good lawyer makes him less eligible for the death penalty. That would be the height of arbitrariness and capriciousness.

But the criminal justice system is a system of human beings, and because it is a system of human beings, there is going to be an inevitable amount of arbitrariness. In the real world, results in death penalty cases can and do hinge on the human element — the varying strengths, weaknesses, and vicissitudes of the judges, jurors, prosecutors, and defense lawyers who participate in the process. Among these, variations in the quality of defense lawyering have particularly profound — and particularly troubling — implications, and this is so because defense lawyers play especially important and distinctive roles in the process. Capital defense lawyers face daunting responsibilities unlike those encountered in any other dimension of criminal practice. There is a multitude of stages in every death case, and in each stage there are so many challenging decisions that have to be made, each with the potential to spell the difference between a life sentence or a death verdict. Lawyers make these decisions with varying skill and sophistication. When the decisions are not made as well as they could be, the consequences can be downright fatal because, given the rules that courts follow, a lawyer's poor handling of one of these decisions is very difficult to undo or remedy later. The upshot is arbitrariness in the administration of the death penalty. The very same issue might arise in two different capital cases, with the issue being well handled by the defense lawyer in one of these cases and not so well handled by the defense lawyer in the other. In the former, the defendant profits from good fortune and secures a life sentence; in the latter, the defendant suffers a death sentence. Seen in this light, the system begins to appear uncomfortably like a lottery.

The problem in fact runs deeper. As many previous speakers have noted, much of the Eighth Amendment capital punishment law that has become so notoriously complicated exists to guard against arbitrariness owing to the vicissitudes of judges, jurors, and prosecutors. The legal system depends on lawyers to employ these laws, and many of them do it well, many of them do it poorly, and many of them fair to middling. Rules designed to protect against discrimination, for instance, have to be raised by the defense lawyer. If these protections are not invoked by counsel — or if they are invoked poorly by counsel — they will not be observed in that case, and will lose their effectiveness. Arbitrariness is thus compounded.

Further exacerbating the problem is the fact that while capital defense lawyering has become a highly specialized form of legal practice, the legal system still calls on generalists to undertake the responsibility. Almost all capitally charged defendants are indigent. It is the very rare defendant who has the money to hire a lawyer of the stature and skill of Wade and Roger Smith, to name but two of the most prominent members of North Carolina's criminal defense bar.

The vast majority of capital defendants are represented by court-appointed lawyers, and truth is that our system for providing court-appointed representation is not built to provide lawyers who have the specialized training, experience, and skill necessary for the unique challenges of modern capital litigation. Rather, the existing system is designed to provide lawyers for the run-of-the-mill criminal docket — a high-volume docket that moves quickly and which disposes of well over 90 percent of its relatively uncomplicated cases by negotiation or plea without trial. That does not describe today's complex, specialized death-penalty practice.

There was a time — am not sure exactly when the time ended — when inadequacies and inequalities in lawyering could be masked. The reason why they could be masked is that federal habeas corpus existed in a way that it does not today.* Time was when federal courts stood open to review capital cases closely and conscientiously, when they were willing to hear complaints and to face issues that may not have been perfectly presented earlier. Before an individual could go to his or her death, the case had to survive a searching examination in the federal courts, where good attorneys could be provided to ensure an equality of treatment and to detect and undo the arbitrariness that might have crept into the case at an earlier stage. Many of you know that the habeas corpus to which I am alluding is not the habeas corpus we have today. Decisions by the Rehnquist Court for more than a decade, coupled with the negative contributions of the Congress elected in 1994, have cut back substantially on federal corpus review, leaving it but a shadow of what it was ten to fifteen years ago. Arbitrariness that once might have been corrected by the federal courts now goes unremedied.

Nor does the constitutional promise of "effective assistance of counsel," made by the Sixth Amendment, operate meaningfully today

*See Glossary, page 87.

to guard against the arbitrariness that stems from poor and desperate capital defense lawyering. Simply put, the Supreme Court's standard for constitutionally effective assistance of counsel — set forth in *Strickland v. Washington* — is especially forgiving of poor lawyering. A day does not pass when a capital defense lawyer provides regrettably weak service to a defendant, but it is also a fairly rare day when that capital defense lawyer is found to be have provided *unconstitutionally ineffective* counsel such that a death sentence must be set aside.

Now the ABA has recognized all this, and recognized that it is unforgivable. It is particularly unforgivable because much of it can be corrected. It will take money.* Perhaps more important, it will take commitment — a commitment to actually deliver the justice that is promised, explicitly and implicitly, by the United States Constitution, and the Constitution's Sixth and Eighth Amendments in particular. At bottom, the ABA challenges America to keep its promise. To America, the ABA says, "If you continue to claim that you can have a capital punishment system that is truly legitimate, truly decent, then pay for it, provide for it. And until you do, you should put a halt to executions."

TYE HUNTER

What are the things that make for a fair trial? I'd say there are three — you could list a hundred, but I would boil them down to three. The first is an impartial judge. The second is an intelligent and fair jury. And the third is a roughly equal advocacy — roughly equal

---

*But perhaps not as much as what prosecution of capital cases is costing taxpayers in total, especially since Congress passed the crime bill of 1994 authorizing the federal death penalty to a wider range of criminals; the number of death cases sanctioned by the U. S. Attorney General increased from five in 1993 to thirty-one in 1997. According to a 1998 report by the Judicial Conference of the United States, which represents federal judges, defending someone in a death-penalty case costs an average of $218,112. If the death penalty is not sought, the cost is $55,772. Prosecuting death cases costs even more — about $365,000 per defendant.

in resources and ability on both sides. If you have these three things, you have the rough making of a fair trial.

In our panel this afternoon we're talking about the third thing.

We do not have roughly equal advocacy. I'm not talking about having great defense lawyers. I'm talking about having defense lawyers who are roughly as good as senior assistant district attorneys, as the district attorneys in North Carolina. The fact is, defense lawyers are not as well trained, they're not as well prepared, they're not as motivated, and they don't do as good a job, by and large, as the prosecuting district attorneys. There are notable exceptions, some of whom are in this room, but the exceptions are few. So, the fundamental idea that a trial is a fair way at arriving at a decision really depends on that rough equality, and it simply doesn't exist in North Carolina criminal courts.

How do we evaluate the quality of advocacy — after a case is decided? We may ask, "Was this a fair trial or not?" But do we review the case and ask, "Was there a rough equality in the ability of the lawyering?." We do not.

I look at the way we evaluate the medical profession. Say, somebody dies on the operating table who shouldn't have died. Consider the resources and the criticisms that are brought to bear on the medical profession. Doctors may have made good grades in college and graduated from medical school, but they're capable of having bad days and making terrible mistakes. So I think it appropriate that whenever preventable medical tragedies occur, cases are examined and questions asked, to see if in fact these trained professionals, who are competent in 90 percent of the things they do and on 90 percent of their days, may not have got caught on a bad day and made a terrible, possibly fatal mistake.

This is not the kind of review we do of lawyers after capital cases. Basically, the question, "Was the lawyer bad or good enough?" is the same as asking, "Would the defendant have been as well or better served if he had had no lawyer at all?" If we evaluated surgeons in this way, the question would be, "Was it bad enough that the patient would have been as well or better served if the surgeon had never been there?" But that's the base-line test for evaluating lawyers after a capital trial.

And there are two reasons for this. One is, all kinds of people get operated on, whereas the individuals on that death penalty table tend to be a pretty exclusive group, a group that people generally aren't that concerned about. A lot of people feel that if the crime is bad enough, you don't deserve a fair trial; that this insistence on a fair trial or a good lawyer is wrongheaded.

And the second reason is, there is a lot of self-protection. Lawyers are very reluctant to criticize other lawyers. They don't mind chopping up the local doctor in little bitty pieces; that's part of their professional responsibility. But when it comes to lawyers — there are lawyers in almost every county that the other lawyers in that county wouldn't hire to represent them for a speeding ticket. And yet these incompetents are on the capital appointed list. These lawyers are trying cases where people's lives are at stake. If they were doctors performing brain surgery, nobody who knew them would let them even give booster shots. And yet, when we go back through cases after the fact and look at the performances of the lawyers, the question we ask isn't, "Was this a fair trial, were there equivalent advocates?" The question we ask, in effect, is "Would the defendant have been better off with no lawyer at all?" We have a terrible problem.

Under our current law there is really no good way to look at the issue of lawyer effectiveness. I think there are a lot of things just about the nature of small community practice, which is the predominant practice in North Carolina, that inhibits effective evaluation. If you watch TV shows about lawyers, you'll notice that all the lawyers except Matlock are based in big cities, and these lawyers and these district attorneys are shown going after each other, hammer and tongs. They don't live in the same neighborhood. They don't meet at the golf course. They don't go to the same churches. But here in North Carolina most of our criminal defense lawyers live and practice in small communities. I'd say that in ninety of our one hundred counties the kind of law practiced is the lawyering of accommodation and relationship: "I'll be reasonable in this case if you'll be reasonable," and everybody getting along. I'm not saying that's a bad thing. I think maybe it's a good thing in a lot of respects, but it hardly prepares you for a high-profile homicide case when one comes along. When that happens, it's not going to be a matter of saying, "Since we play golf together on Saturday, you're going to treat me and my client right." The mutual back-scratching is over. Capital cases just require an entirely different way of practicing, but we still evaluate the lawyers who practice it as if it's all right and enough for them to be ranked and scored by their fraternity brothers.

I don't blame lawyers entirely for this situation. In many ways the death penalty is a public-policy decision that non-lawyers — the Legislature, the citizens — have made, and it's being done on the backs of lawyers. The Chief Justice said 70 percent of the Court's time was devoted to the death-penalty issue — not because the judges thought that reviewing our death penalty system was worth 70 percent of their time but simply because we have a lot of death-penalty cases and each one requires careful review. On the other hand, the decision that North Carolina have so many death-penalty cases was made by people who don't have to carry it out.

The death penalty has had a terribly distorted effect on both the courts and the practice of law in North Carolina. I think it's really been quite destructive to our legal system, and continues to be.

GRETCHEN ENGEL
Attorney, Center for Death Penalty Litigation, Durham

When the ABA resolution was first passed, I got a lot of letters from clients wanting me to explain it to them. Lots of them had the mistaken idea that somehow the ABA resolution meant that their death sentence would not be carried out. They all wanted to know. "What does it mean?" And my short answer was, "It doesn't mean a damn thing." The long answer, however, is that it's a step in a process. Some day, when the death penalty is outlawed in the United States, we will look back on the ABA resolution and say, "That was an important step in the right direction."

Another step was taken when Justice Blackmun wrote his dissent in *Callins v. Collins,* in which he said, "I shall no longer tinker with the machinery of death." I went back to look at his dissent, and also at what the ABA resolution had to say about competency of counsel. What Justice Blackmun talked about was how, in every capital case that's tried, we hope the defendant whose life is at risk will be represented by competent counsel and that this counsel will investigate all aspects of the case. And what the ABA resolution says is, "Let's provide standards that counsel will have to adhere to. We must improve the quality of representation." At some level what I want to say is that this kind of tinkering is not going to do it. It's just not going to solve the problem.

A case comes to mind; I'll refer to it as the Billy Patrick case. This was not one of those cases where, to draw on the record and my own observation, the person was represented by an attorney who'd started preparing only two weeks before the trial. Billy Patrick was not defended, as was true in another case I remember, by an attorney who had been found guilty of receiving kiddie porn and everybody in the whole county knew it. It wasn't a case where the co-counsel had never done a jury trial before. It wasn't a case where a white attorney consistently referred to black people, including his clients, in terms of racial stereotypes that most people would find offensive.

True, the attorney was white and Billy Patrick was black. The prosecutors were white, the chief investigative officers were white, the judge was white, and the jurors were white. There is that part of it. But this was a case where the lawyer was excellent. He was one of the best attorneys in the state. In the previous seven or eight homicide cases that he had represented defendants against this district attorney, he had won either an acquittal or had beaten back the state's call for death. Then he got this case. He got an investigator, he sent the investigator out of state to talk with members of the defendant's family, he hired experts. He did his job.

Now, he had to get going fast, because the crime happened in August and went to trial in December of the same year. The district attorney scheduled that; North Carolina, as you may know, is the only state in the country where district attorneys control the calendar and are able to set when cases will be tried. And because the judge's schedule is already preprinted in six-month segments, that means that if the district attorney is of a mind to, he or she can select the judge who will preside over the case. And that's exactly what happened in this case.

This was a bad case. It was a stabbing, very brutal, of a mother and a child. One of the significant issues was the time of death, when the crime occurred. The victims were last seen around midnight on a Sunday night. The bodies were found Tuesday morning. So it had to have happened either Sunday night or Monday night. The defendant had an airtight alibi for Monday and Monday night. The state's theory was that the crime happened sometime Sunday night, that it happened between 3 AM when the defendant gets back to the apartment complex, and 7, maybe 6 AM, when he goes to work. But what the state hid for fifteen years was that someone saw the victim at 4:45 in the morning. At trial, the defense attorney pressed constantly, "I want to know, what does law enforcement know about when people last saw this victim?" At some point during the trial, notes of the statement by the witness — who came forward two days after the bodies were discovered — and had seen the mother alive at 4:45 — were given to the judge privately for him to read. At that point, that judge, who had been selected by the district attorney, said "I don't see any reason to give this over to you."

I have no doubt that if this information had been available to this attorney, as good as he was he certainly would not have gotten the death penalty for his client. As bad as this murder was, this was a jury that was actively considering a life sentence. The jurors asked about parole, "What's the meaning of a life sentence?" they wanted to know. The judge told them, "You don't have to worry about that." Billy Patrick might have even gotten a mistrial, an acquittal. But now he's in federal habeas, and with the procedural obstacles referred to earlier, the chances of relief are extremely limited.

I look at a case like this and I think, here you have this great lawyer, and what do you do? You still have a very unfair trial.

I began by saying that tinkering isn't going to do anything. And now I'm going to contradict myself and give you three suggestions for what I think would have made a difference, in this case and in other cases. All the things that were brought to bear in this case — prosecutorial misconduct, a judge who was not impartial — these things are even more compelling and determining when you don't have the advocate, when you don't have the equality between the advocates that was referred to earlier. Something has to be done to adjust these things.

To go back to Justice Blackmun: Right after he talks about our hope for competent counsel, he says, "We also would hope that the defendant would appear before a judge who is committed to the protection of the defendant's rights." And in the same vein, "We would hope that the prosecution, in urging the penalty of death, will have exercised its discretion wisely, free from bias, prejudice, or political motive, and will be humble, rather than be emboldened by the awesome authority conferred by the state."

I think the only ways to make these things happen are: Number One, to take away the calendaring power of the district attorney in North Carolina, so that a district attorney can not wield that power to secure the result this one did in this case and doubtlessly in other cases, just by selecting the judge and by scheduling one capital case after another. When there is a small number of people on the court-appointed list for capital cases, the attorneys do not have the time, even if they're well-intentioned, to prepare the cases adequately. They simply cannot do it. The DA can use his calendaring power to ride roughshod over the defense attorney. So I think that's Number One.

Number Two is to mandate open file discovery so we don't have this game of "Well, do they know something the defense doesn't know." Open up those files, so you really do have an even playing field with the information. If we count strictly on the hope that prosecutors will do their duty — to seek justice and not only conviction — in many cases we're going to be disappointed.

And last, we might think about a statewide capital trial unit, where you have specialized people doing these cases. As the ABA points out, ordinary professional qualifications are inadequate. This is a very specialized field. Also, by having a unit of people who're trained, you in some ways redress the power differential between the prosecutor's office, which is specialized, which has that special relationship with the local judge; you have another body to confront these two on a more equal basis. Such a unit could guarantee defendants more equal access to expert services, to investigative services, so that the defendant is not dependent on the whims of the local judge, who may or may not want to give money to help a person accused of a heinous crime in his community.

If we're going to have the death penalty, this is the kind of tinkering I think we have to do. We can at least make it so that these horrific results don't occur.

Panel V
"What does it mean?"
McNeill Smith Jr., Moderator
Senior Partner, Smith Helms Mullis & Moore, Greensboro

One of the members of the ABA's executive committee says that he's a great believer in the death penalty. He says it serves to release tensions in people, that it makes them feel that justice is being done. He would like to see to see more executions, and I think he's serious.

So on this issue we have many points of view. I found especially interesting what criminal defense lawyers told us at a meeting of the Individual Rights section. Prosecutors didn't show up at this meeting in any significant number, so it was pretty much dominated by the criminal defense lawyers. Almost to a man, these criminal defense lawyers agreed that the problem was not with the death penalty as such but with the variation in the way cases are tried, from judge to judge, from county to county. They were all of the opinion that in North Carolina the prosecution of death-penalty cases is a very fractious thing.

The Honorable Harry Martin
North Carolina Supreme Court Justice Emeritus

Chief Justice Jim Exum was correct when he said earlier today that the courts had done about all they could do concerning the death penalty. The lawyers through all their ingenuity have about exhausted the possibilities for getting something done about its constitutionality. There will be idiosyncratic cases along the way, where relief can be gained from the courts because of some violation of the Constitution. But insofar as having the death penalty declared unconstitutional, I don't believe that's going to happen, at least not in the near future.

I think we have to look now to the political process. I do not believe that moral arguments will be persuasive to the various people in the political process, such as administration leaders and members of various state and federal legislatures. The approach has to come from some other way.

It is not politically expedient for politicians to say, "If you elect me or re-elect me to the General Assembly I will introduce a bill to abolish the death penalty." That person is not going to be elected.

I don't mean that we should abandon moral arguments about the validity of the death penalty. But from a practical standpoint we've got to get the people who make the public policy of the state and the nation to look at something more attractive, something that voters appreciate. So what is selling today to the voter? As I read the newspapers, what is selling to the voters is, "Reduce costs of government." That's one thing, and as part of that, "Reduce taxes."

The judicial branch of government spends a minuscule part of the total budget. In North Carolina I think the judicial budget is less than 3 percent of the total budget. In dollars, though, it is a considerable amount of money, because the total budget is now up in the billions — maybe twelve or fourteen billion dollars. So, to the man in the street what's allocated to the judiciary is a considerable amount of money.

Now, fortunately in North Carolina a study has been made of the cost of the death penalty as administered. The study was made in 1991 and 1992 by Duke University under a contract to the administrative office of the court. Justice Exum, who was the chief justice during that period, was instrumental in having the study done. The data show that the death penalty is economically unsound and as a consequence we now can make a convincing case to the legislature that taxpayers would be saved an enormous amount of money by abolishing it.

A few figures: It costs $84,000 to try a capital case, whether the person is sentenced to execution or life imprisonment. To try a non-capital case, it costs about $17,000. Roughly, in round figures, since the death penalty was held constitutional by the U. S. Supreme Court — about 1976 or thereabouts — we have tried about 4,000 capital cases in North Carolina. $84,000 times 4,000 is $336 million. That's a sizeable amount of money, and that's only the trial part.

This doesn't include the cost of appeals. Nor does it include post-conviction costs, which average about $255,000 per death penalty. The average cost per execution in North Carolina — and we've executed nine people since the death penalty became constitutional — is $2.16 million. Multiply that figure by nine and you get roughly $19 million. That's what these nine executions have cost taxpayers. Now, there are 177 people on Death Row at this time. Just the cost of putting them there, not counting post conviction costs, is $39,160,000.

I cite these statistics to demonstrate how people who build public policy can approach their constituents and say, "I'm going to vote for this bill to abolish the death penalty because it's going to save you money." Politicians are not going to win votes by saying, "I'm going to vote to abolish the death penalty because it's wrong and doesn't belong in our society." It's an unusual voter out there who's going to buy that argument. But talk to him about dollars and show him how much the death penalty is costing him, and —.

JULIUS CHAMBERS
Chancellor, North Carolina Central University

I have the greatest admiration for Judge Martin, but I don't think a dollar appeal is going to sell very much in this venue. There are other things motivating people. We are building more prisons than we can ever imagine, and nobody worries. It certainly costs more to build a prison than it does to give a child a dollar to learn how to make a living and stay out of prison. There's something at work in our culture that's much more fundamental than money and taxes.

Once, years ago, Justice Marshall talked about how we express our immorality, or our lack of consideration of people, in a number of different ways. I don't think you can look at capital punishment without looking at what's happening with children in the schools, without looking at people hunting for jobs, without looking at the pervasiveness of racism in this country and what we're doing with poor people. We see differences in the treatment of poor people and not even raise an eyebrow. Most of us have had very little to say about welfare reform and its effects. I find this amazing. All these things intertwine. You can't separate them. I don't know how the North Carolinians Against the Death Penalty can expect to have much major impact without looking at, or forcing somebody to look at, all the other things that are going on in this state and in this country that are killing people and debasing our spirit.

It's interesting to see how so few people get concerned when we talk about putting somebody to death. We aren't reaching anybody. I look around this audience, and I think I see one black person. Why is that?

We have to think about how to expand our outreach. For example, at the Legal Defense Fund we argued that capital punishment was being used primarily against black people. To a degree — to a significant degree — that was true. But I think the more significant group affected is poor people. I don't know how many people you can count with any money who have been put to death by the state. Why is that?

Look at the people put to death. They are all poor people. Of all colors, but poor. Maybe we ought to do something to get the country to think more about poor people.

This Legislature over there. Some of us go over there to lobby for legislation to help schoolchildren get health care. We start off talking about how we reduce taxes and we'd be over there a year from now and poor children still wouldn't have any health care. You go to Raleigh and start talking about abolishing capital punishment, or just adhering to the ABA recommendation, and people will think you're crazy.

In his comment on the capital punishment case out of Georgia, Justice Brennan said that how we treat poor people as criminals reflects the real values of America. That's true. I believe, Judge Martin, that this is a real moral issue. We've got to start pushing this idea, not just as it applies to in capital punishment, but across the whole spectrum. We've got to speak out on all the interconnecting issues to do with poverty and race and jobs and health and education because our failure to do so will affect what we're trying to do in a specific area, like abolishing capital punishment. I don't think we're going to have much impact until we do.

I must tell you in closing, I've practiced law for a long time. I have never been so disappointed in our federal court system as in the past five years. Somebody said something about following precedents. The courts don't worry about precedents. They decide what they want to decide. I don't think they follow facts, either. And we don't yell much, you and I, about what the courts are doing — again, not just in the criminal capital punishment area but in criminal law, in housing, health care, and all the rest.

All of us have got to start yelling more.

W.W. FINLATOR

Reverend Emeritus, Pullen Memorial Baptist Church, Raleigh

I'm in the presence of so many high legal intellects that I feel diminished. For comfort, I keep reminding myself that a dwarf on the shoulders of a giant can see farther than the giant.

I'm old enough now to be on my guard against being historical and telling old tales, but I'm remembering that some twenty-five years ago a man named Paul Green came to Raleigh to Central Prison on the eve of every capital punishment case and stood alone saying nothing. This came to be known as the lonely vigil. I'm remembering a man named Marion Wright, a colleague, a man who lived up in the mountains, a great defender of civil rights. He and Paul were largely responsible for starting this organization.* Twenty-five years ago, money was much more than it is now. Marion Wright came to Chapel Hill one time and spent the night with Paul Green. It was at a time when Paul was trying to get the money to start this organization. Marion came away and warned all of us that if Paul Green invites you to spend the night with him it'll cost you a hundred dollars.

I want to thank the ABA for what it's done. I almost want to call it a moraltorium. There's a great story about this young law student and a case was coming up that involved some cynicism. This young student said, "Well, Professor, is that right?" And the professor said: "Is it right? If you're interested in right and wrong, you should transfer to the theological seminary."

Well, there's a lady in the audience who asked me, "Why don't you say something about the responsibility of the church?" She means the mainline Protestant and Catholic churches because the evangelical fundamentalist Baptists are all in favor of capital punishment. "Why don't the people of the Protestant mainline churches and Catholic churches — why don't they force their ministers to preach sermons on capital punishment?" May we all go home and do that, because with all due reverence for the judge over here, this is a moral issue, a matter of principle.

There was a Supreme Court justice who died not long ago. People were discussing pornography. He was not in favor of pornography, but he was in favor of the government staying away from it because the government has no right to say what we can read or see. The

*North Carolinians Against the Death Penalty

antipornography lobby showed a video, a very immoral video. Most of the justices went to see it, but he scorned it. "I don't need to see it. I know what pornography is. You can't make me feel different about it. I'm just against government censorship." I think that's what we've got to do about capital punishment. You can't move people anyway except on principle, and you have to come out and say, "We're one hundred percent against it no matter how atrocious, no matter how heinous the crime — we're against it lock, stock, and barrel."

Here's this lady who was executed recently in Texas. She had the pope intercede for her. She had Jerry Falwell intercede for her. She had Pat Robertson intercede for her. She was white, she was a lady, and she was a born-again Christian. All that, some said, should have made a difference. That's not operating on principle. And now we have Secretary of State Madeleine Albright saying, "Yes, better not execute this Paraguayan because of the repercussions." Here again we're not operating on principle. We have Mrs. Billy Graham coming to Raleigh week after week visiting this lady who was going to be executed. Here was a beautiful relationship, but Mrs. Graham never said one word about capital punishment itself. Of course she couldn't afford to. She would hurt Billy Graham's great mission. This is not operating on principle.

So, with you, I am going to hope that we can change the Supreme Court in spite of what has been said. Remember, it has changed. I think ultimately, if we work at it, we can change the Court again.

At this point the Court doesn't know it, but it's acting lawlessly. The United States has signed a treaty with the United Nations that before we execute any foreigner within our borders we see to it that he is in touch with his ambassador, that he's in touch with his people back home. But when the state of Virginia decided to kill a Paraguayan, the Supreme Court looked the other way. It was just determined to carry on this ugly, ugly affair. Well folks, let me ask you to join me and let me have the honor to join you, and let's do all we can on the principle that the whole thing is just — tacky.

STEPHEN DEAR
People of Faith Against the Death Penalty

I see great signs of hope that the death penalty is going to be abolished. It's just a matter of time. Look at Europe. Estonia can't join the European Union if it has the death penalty, so Estonia abolishes the death penalty. Except for the reference to the sentencing of the Paraguayan in Virginia, I haven't heard anybody here today say anything about the international pressure that's growing on the United States. There's a bill before the European Union that calls for no company to build a plant in an American state that has the death penalty. When a group of religious leaders met with Governor Hunt in January, before Ricky Sanderson was executed, this was brought up. Hunt got very upset about it, about that prospect, even though it might not be binding. And last summer, when Joseph Odell was executed in Virginia — I don't know how many people in this room ever heard of Joseph Odell, but five million people in Italy were troubled enough to watch their Italian reporters go to Richmond and cover his execution. He's now buried in Italy. There's a lot of pressure, a lot of interest around the world in executions in the United States. I'm wondering, how can we, how can the ABA, link into that? Maybe we could bring people from Europe over here to speak to us.

MCNEILL SMITH

I don't think we can count on the ABA to do anything but raise questions.

JULIUS CHAMBERS

That's a good suggestion. People in the United States don't know what's happening in other countries with capital punishment. One of the things we might do is educate people as to what's happening around the world. The other thing is, we haven't taken advantage of the different, all the existing, treaties and international agreements.

Voice from Audience

My brother is on Death Row. This morning, during the first panel, Mr. Dayan said that every person on Death Row is a poor person who has been abused and has no means. That is not the case with my brother. He had the means to hire an attorney, a private attorney. He's an educated man, he was an officer in the Army, he had a wonderful childhood. He had the means of a white person. He got railroaded just like anybody else. As you were saying, the rural jury where he was tried, the people were very ignorant. He was not known, he was new to that area, and the DA presented him as a monster. "Look at him," he'd say to the jury. "He's a monster." The way he lied about him, even myself, if I hadn't known him as my brother, I would have thought him a monster. The power of the DA is absolutely criminal. My brother was sent to Death Row, and right after he was convicted to death, one of the jurors — we were outside the courtroom — said to the DA, "When are we going to get our check for this trial?" It was a two-month trial. That was right in front of us, the defendant's family, and it was disgusting.

Julius Chambers

Again, I think — if we seriously mean to ensure that people in whatever walk of life have an equal chance — we will have to tie efforts to abolish capital punishment with other educational efforts aimed at ending discrimination, poverty, and the privilege of class.

DAN POLLITT

We're hoping that as a result of this meeting today the trial lawyers, and the regular bar, will adopt resolutions and send them along to the Legislature. We're asking for something very modest. We have a petition that recites the concerns of the American Bar Association, and then reads: "We urge the General Assembly to appoint a committee to study whether these concerns are valid in North Carolina, whether a moratorium on executions is required in the name of equal protection and due process." We made several copies, so you should find room on one of them for your signature. Thank you all for coming.

THE PANELISTS

Melvin "Skip" Alston is president of the North Carolina State Conference of NAACP Branches, having been elected in 1997 with 63 percent of the votes in a four-man race. A native of Durham, he was educated in the Durham public schools and at North Carolina Central University, majoring in business administration. He moved to Greensboro in 1979 and there, at twenty-five, founded S&J Management Corporation, a real estate firm specializing in property management and sales. The corporation currently has eighteen full-time employees and manages properties in the Greensboro area valued at more than $45 million. He is a member of the Guilford County Board of Commissioners and served for four years as treasurer of the National Association of Black County Officials.

Frank Ballance is an eight-term state senator from the Second District (Warren County) and is the Senate's elected Deputy President *Pro Tem*. He has introduced bills to abolish the death penalty, to abolish the death penalty for juveniles, and to abolish the death penalty for the mentally ill. In 1998 he was the recipient of the prestigious Frank Porter Graham Award for "advancing civil liberties in North Carolina."

Lou Bilionis, a former assistant Appellate Defender, teaches constitutional law at the University of North Carolina, where he also conducts a seminar on the death penalty. As an undergraduate at UNC-Chapel Hill, he was a Moorehead Scholar and editor of the Daily Tar Heel.

Jack Boger is a professor and associate dean at the University of North Carolina School of Law. He has served as the director of the NAACP Legal Defense Fund Death Penalty Project and has argued

81

several Supreme Court cases, including the landmark *McCleskey v. Kemp*. In addition to an A.B. from Duke and a J. D. from UNC, he holds a Masters of Divinity degree from Yale.

Julius Chambers was graduated in 1958 from North Carolina Central University summa cum laude with a B.A. in history. Since January 1, 1993 he has been NCCCU's chancellor. During the years between, he earned a law degree from UNC-Chapel Hill, established the first integrated law firm in North Carolina (in Charlotte, with James Ferguson and Adam Stein), and served for nine years as director-counsel of the NAACP Legal Defense and Educational Fund in New York City. As a student at the UNC School of Law, he was first in the class of '62 and elected by his peers, all white, to the editorship of the Law Review, becoming the first African American to hold this title at any historically white law school in the South. He holds seven honorary LL.D. degrees and counts among his many other honors the 1994 Courageous Advocacy Award of the American College of Trial Lawyers, the Columbia University Medal for Excellence, and the ACLU's Frank Porter Graham Award.

Marshall Dayan began his law practice with the Mississippi ACLU Delta Death-Penalty Project and then joined the North Carolina Center for Death Penalty Litigation. He has represented Death Row inmates for twelve years. In 1988 his commitment and energy on their behalf won him the Paul Green Award.

Gretchen Engel is a graduate of Oberlin College and Northeastern Law School. To date her entire professional career has been spent as staff attorney at the Center for Death Penalty Litigation, which she joined in 1992. She has participated in a dozen or more capital cases.

James Exum Jr. has served as a member of the General Assembly, a Superior Court judge, and chief justice of the North Carolina Supreme Court. Upon retirement in 1995, he taught briefly at the UNC School of Law. He is now a senior partner in the Greensboro firm of Smith, Helms, Mullis & Moore. He has been honored with the Frank Porter Graham Award.

W. W. Finlator is pastor emeritus of Raleigh's Pullen Memorial Church. He has ministered to inmates at Central Prison for many years. He has chaired the North Carolina Advisory Committee to the United States Civil Rights Commission and has also served as vice president of the American Civil Liberties Union. His work has won him many citations, including the ACLU's Frank Porter Graham Award.

Henderson Hill, a vice president of the North Carolina Academy of Trial Lawyers, teaches a death penalty seminar at Duke. He is a partner in the Charlotte firm of Ferguson, Stein, Wallas, Adkins, Graham & Sumter. He formerly directed the Center for Death Penalty Litigation and is the 1999 recipient of the Paul Green Award.

Tye Hunter is the North Carolina Appellate Defender and as such litigates at all levels many of the state's death penalty cases. Generous with his time and talents, he is active as on the boards of many socially oriented organizations.

Verla Insko represents the Twenty-fourth District (Orange County) in the North Carolina General Assembly. She serves on the legislature's Domestic Violence Study Commission and has introduced a bill to amend the state Constitution to recognize the right to health care as an essential safeguard of human life and dignity. She is a former county commissioner.

Ellie Kinnaird, a former Councilwoman and Mayor of Carrboro, is now a North Carolina state senator, where she has distinguished herself as vice chair of the Women's Caucus and chair of the State and Local Government Committee. A leader in the movement to declare a moratorium on the death penalty, she brings to her public statements both passion and hard facts. Among the facts she has found most persuasive among her constitutents: that (1) more than 80 innocent people have been freed from Death Row since the reintroduction of capital punishment in the 1970s and (2) most North Carolina police chiefs consider the death penalty an ineffective tool for law enforcement.

Tom Loflin is a leading defense lawyer in Durham. He recently appeared before the European Commission on Human Rights, arguing that it was wrong under the International Convention on Human Rights for England to try an eleven-year-old boy as an adult, no matter how heinous the crime.

Harry Martin was elected time and again to the Superior Court of North Carolina and then to the Supreme Court. After reaching the age of mandatory retirement, he has taught a popular seminar at the UNC School of Law and been in private practice with his son in Hillsborough.

Mickey Michaux is representative to the General Assembly from Durham. In 1975 he led the fight to abolish the death penalty. He succeeded in having it banned for rape, burglary, and arson — but not for murder. He has kept at it ever since.

Barry Nakell, a retired professor from the UNC School of Law, is the author of the pioneer study of the death penalty as applied in North Carolina: *The Arbitrariness of the Death Penalty.* He has represented defendants accused of murder at all levels of trial and appeal. He is a recipient of the ACLU annual Frank Porter Graham award.

Daniel Pollitt is a retired professor from the UNC School of Law. *See "About the Editors," p. 121.*

Ken Rose is the director of the Center for Death Penalty Litigation in Durham. He has been a hands-on participant in many capital cases, winning a significant number of them at every level of litigation, from the United States Supreme Court on down.

McNeill Smith is a senior partner in the law firm of Smith, Helms, Mullis & Moore. He is known nationally for his trial ability and for his leadership in the Individual Rights Section of the American Bar Association. He was the initial chair of the North Carolina Advisory Committee to the United States Civil Rights Commission and was a principal organizer of the North Carolina Civil Liberties Union. He too is a recipient of the Frank Porter Graham Award.

Adam Stein is a senior partner in Ferguson, Stein, Wallas, Adkins, Gresham, and Sumter. He cut his legal teeth representing juveniles charged with murder and with Julius Chambers blazed the legal trail for human rights and racial justice. A former State Appellate Defender, he is a past president of the North Carolina Academy of Trial Lawyers. He holds a Frank Porter Graham Award.

Andrew Short, Ph. D., a Charlotte psychologist, is a leader in the ongoing effort to end the death penalty for the mentally retarded.

Faye Sultan is director of University Psychological Associates in Charlotte. She began her career as a staff psychologist at the Women's Prison in Raleigh. She is called on frequently as an expert witness in death penalty cases, not only in North Carolina but throughout the South.

GLOSSARY

*A guide to relevant Constitutional provisions
and Supreme Court decisions*

By Dan Pollitt

THE CONSTITUTION

The Fifth Amendment provides in pertinent part that "no person" shall be deprived of "life, liberty, or property without *due process of law.*" The Fourteenth Amendment has a similar provision. Both amendments were designed to curb various forms of governmental abuse, unfairness, and oppression.

The Sixth Amendment provides in part that in all criminal prosecutions the accused shall "have the *assistance of counsel* for his defense." This means "competent" counsel.

The Eighth Amendment provides that "excessive bail shall not be required, nor excessive fines imposed, nor cruel and unusual punishments inflicted." In the case of *Trop v. Dulles*, 356 U.S. 86 (1958), the Supreme Court explained "The basic concept underlying the Eighth Amendment is nothing less than the dignity of man....The words of the Amendment are not precise and their scope is not static. The Amendment must draw its meaning from the evolving standards of decency that mark the progress of a maturing society." The Court applies "the evolving standards of decency" not by its own subjective standards, but rather by reference to state laws on the subject and, when possible, to jury verdicts.

The Fourteenth Amendment provides in part that "no state shall deny to any person within its jurisdiction *the equal protection of the laws.*" It is intended to eliminate discrimination on the basis of race, color, gender, national origin, and the like.

Habeas Corpus. A writ of habeas corpus (literally, "to have the body") is the Latin name for a process whereby a court commands a jailer to justify the continued confinement of the person seeking the writ. Typically, a person condemned to death will contend that his conviction is unconstitutional because of his youth (due process), his insanity (cruel and unusual punishment), his race (equal protection), the inadequacy of counsel, or a combination of these issues. When the writ is served on the warden, he or she must respond to these contentions.

THE SUPREME COURT CASES

The Beginning. *McGautha v. California*, 402 U.S. 183 (1971). This case describes the situation that prevailed throughout the United States in 1971. McGautha was convicted of murder in California, and under state law the penalty was left to the jury's discretion. The jury was told that it could be "governed by mere sentiment and sympathy" for the accused, that it was entirely free to act according to its own "judgment, conscience, and absolute discretion." When the jury sentenced him to death, McGautha appealed. He contended that for the jury to be given absolute discretion to impose the death penalty "as it sees fit" violates the command of the Fourteenth Amendment that "no state shall deprive a person of his life without due process of law." The jury's action, he maintained, was therefore lawless. By a vote of six to three, the Supreme Court rejected the claim — in part because history shows there were "compassionate purposes" behind allowing juries to decide the penalty, in part because every state with the death penalty followed this model, and in part because of the difficulty providing workable standards to guide the jury's discretion.

The Abolition. *Furman v. Georgia*, 408 U.S. 238 (1972). Here the Supreme Court outlawed the death penalty. Furman, a grade-school drop-out, was diagnosed as "mentally deficient, mild to moderate, with psychiatric episodes associated with convulsive disorders." He killed a householder during a burglary and a Georgia jury sentenced him to death. The jury, as in the *McGautha* case, had absolute discretion. The Supreme Court voted five to four to reverse the decision in *McGautha* because leaving the penalty to the uncontrolled discretion of the jury violated the "cruel and unusual" prohibition of the Eighth Amendment. Justice Douglas (one of five justices who wrote separate opinions) wrote that under the present system "people live or die on the whim of one man (the judge) or twelve (the jury), and studies show that 'it is the poor, the sick, the ignorant, the powerless who are executed." The death penalty laws, he said, are "pregnant with discrimination and discrimination is not comparable with the idea of equal protection of the laws that is implicit in the ban on 'cruel and unusual punishment.'" Justice Brennan, also in the majority, wrote that "when the punishment of death is inflicted in a trivial number of cases in which it is legally available, the conclusion is virtually inescapable that it is being inflicted arbitrarily. Indeed, it smacks of little more than a lottery system." Moreover, he continued, the death penalty by its severity is "degrading to human dignity" and violates the "cruel and unusual ban of the Eighth Amendment." Justice Stewart cast his vote with the majority, writing that the death penalty is cruel and unusual "in the same way that being struck by lighting is cruel and unusual;" it is "wantonly and freakishly imposed."

The Supreme Court left undecided whether in all circumstances the death penalty was "cruel and unusual." Only Justices Brennan and Marshall voted this way.

The Reimposition. *Gregg v. Georgia,* 428 U.S. 153 (1976). After the *Furman* decision, some thirty-five states rewrote their laws on the death penalty to afford guidance to juries and thereby avoid arbitrary and wanton decisions. Now, four years after *Furman,* the Supreme Court voted seven to two to validate the death penalty as revised by the state legislative bodies, holding that the Georgia statute before it for review adequately responded to the concerns expressed in the 1972 decision.

Typically, Georgia's statute provided for a bifurcated, or two-stage, system of trial and sentence. The jury first was to decide guilt or innocence. If it decided guilt, there was to be a second "sentencing" hearing, at which the defendant could introduce evidence in *mitigation* and the prosecutor evidence of *aggravation*. Mitigating factors could include such circumstances as the youth of the offender, the absence of any prior convictions, the influence of drugs, alcohol, or extreme emotional disturbance, and even circumstances that the offender reasonably believed provided a moral justification for his conduct. Evidence could be admitted at the sentence hearing that might not be admissible in the earlier "guilt" phase of the trial. Further, the jury could not impose the death penalty unless it unanimously agreed that there was at least one of ten "aggravating" circumstances, such as a prior conviction for a capital felony; murder while the defendant was engaged in burglary or arson; murder creating a great risk of death to more than one person; or murder that "is outrageously or wantonly vile, horrible or inhuman."

The revised Georgia law required the state Supreme Court to determine whether the sentence of death in any particular case is "excessive or disproportionate to the penalty imposed in similar cases."

Gregg, a hitchhiker, killed and robbed his benefactors. The jury agreed that the murders were committed while Gregg was engaged in an armed robbery, one of the statutory aggravating factors. He was sentenced to death. The State Supreme Court then studied the case and concluded (as required by the revised law) that the death penalty had not resulted from "prejudice or any other arbitrary factor" and was not "excessive or disproportionate to the death penalty applied in similar cases."

The U. S. Supreme Court held that the death penalty as applied under the new Georgia system was not "cruel or unusual" or otherwise unconstitutional. Justices Brennan and Marshall disagreed and continued to dissent in all subsequent cases.

Rape. *Coker v. Georgia*, 422 U.S. 584 (1977) Here the Supreme Court held seven to two that the death penalty is "cruel and unusual" when it is "grossly out of proportion to the severity of the crime." Coker escaped from a Georgia prison, broke into the home of Mr. and Mrs. Carver, tied Mr. Carver in the bathroom, raped Mrs. Carver, and drove away in the Coker family car. He was apprehended, tried for rape, and sentenced to death.

The Supreme Court reversed the death sentence because it was "grossly disproportionate and excessive punishment" for the rape of an adult woman otherwise unharmed. The Court relied heavily on the fact that Georgia was the only state that still authorized the death penalty for the rape of an adult woman.

Insanity. *Ford v. Wainwright*, 477 U.S. 399 (1986). Here the Supreme Court (seven to two) held that the Eighth Amendment's ban on cruel and unusual punishment prohibits the execution of the insane.

In 1974 a Florida court convicted Ford of murder and sentenced him to death. He was perfectly competent at the trial and at sentencing. But while in custody he exhibited a manifest change in behavior. He had delusions that the Ku Klux Klan was out to get him and that the Klan was holding Senator Kennedy hostage. He referred to himself as Pope John Paul III. A psychiatrist retained by his lawyer evaluated him for more than fourteen months and concluded that he was suffering from "a severe, uncontrollable mental disease which closely resembles paranoid schizophrenia with suicide potential." Ford told a second psychiatrist (called by his lawyer) that he would not be executed because he "owned the prison and could control the Governor through mind waves."

Informed of this by Ford's lawyer, the governor ordered Ford to be examined by three additional psychiatrists. Their conclusion, after thirty minutes, was that Ford was competent to be executed. Ford's lawyer was denied the opportunity to participate in the proceedings. The governor signed a death warrant.

Eventually, the case reached the United States Supreme Court. It held that the Eighth Amendment prohibits execution of the insane and that the due process clause requires that the lawyer for a presumably insane defendant be allowed to participate in the proceedings. Justice Marshall wrote for the Court that:

> Whether its aim be to protect the condemned from fear and pain without comfort or understanding, or to protect the dignity of society from the barbarity of exacting needless vengeance, the restriction finds enforcement in the Eighth Amendment.

Mentally Retarded. *Penry v. Lynaugh*, 492 U.S. 402 (1989). It is "cruel and unusual" to execute the insane, but it is not "cruel and unusual" to execute the mentally retarded. Penry was convicted of murder and rape. At the sentencing hearing it was brought out that although he was twenty-two years old at the time of the crime he had the mental age of a six-year-old and the social maturity (the ability to function in society) of a nine-year-old.

The Supreme Court upheld the death penalty. Justice O'Connor wrote that the Eighth Amendment's prohibition of penalties "which offend our society's evolving standards of decency" is measured by "objective evidence of legislative enactments and the conduct of sentencing juries." There is no "national consensus" against executing the mentally retarded, she continued, because "*Penry* cited only one state statute that explicitly bans the practice and has offered no evidence of the general behavior of juries in this regard." She went on to say, "Opinion surveys indicating strong public opposition to such executions do not establish a sufficient societal consensus."

The Court did say that evidence of mental retardation was a "mitigating" factor that the jury could consider at the sentencing stage.

Youth. *Thompson v. Oklahoma.* 487 U.S. 815 (1988) In this case the Court (five to three) held it unconstitutional to execute a youth who was fifteen at the time of the crime.

In concert with three older persons, Thompson had shot and stabbed his brother-in-law to death. The four then chained a concrete block to the body and threw it into a river. At the "penalty phase" of the trial, the prosecutor introduced color photographs of the body after it bobbed to the surface after a month under water. The jury saw this as the "aggravating factor" that certified the murder as especially "heinous, atrocious, or cruel" and sentenced Thompson to death.

The Supreme Court, however, held that the execution of a fifteen-year-old fell short of the "evolving standards of decency that mark the progress of a maturing society." It based this decision on a review of the relevant state legislative enactments and jury determinations and concluded that the imposition of the death penalty on a fifteen-year-old is "now generally abhorrent to the conscience of the community."

During the following year the Supreme Court again examined state enactments and jury verdicts (the statistics failed to demonstrate a "categorical aversion" to the death penalty for those under sixteen or seventeen) and concluded that it was not "cruel and unusual" for Kentucky to execute a sixteen-year-old [*Stanford v. Kentucky*, 492 U.S. 361 (1989)], or for Missouri to execute a seventeen-year-old [*Wilkins v. Missouri*, 492 U.S. 361 (1989)].

Race. *McCleskey v. Kemp*, 481 U.S. 279 (1987) McCleskey, a black man, was sentenced to death for the murder of a white police officer during the armed robbery of an Atlanta furniture store. On appeal, he argued that as administered in Georgia the death penalty discriminated on the basis of race in violation of the Equal Protection clause of the Fourteenth Amendment and that the persistence of racial discrimination rendered the Georgia statute unconstitutional under the Eighth Amendment.

A study of 2,000 Georgia murder cases showed that the lives of white persons are treasured more highly than the lives of blacks. Those who murdered whites were eleven times more likely to receive sentence of death than were those who killed blacks. Twenty-two percent of blacks who murdered whites were sentenced to death, while only 3 percent of white defendants who murdered blacks faced capital sentences. When a white person killed a white person, the death sentence was imposed in 8 percent of the cases; when a black killed a black it was imposed in only 1 percent.

The Court, in a five-to-four decision, accepted the accuracy of these statistics but held that they were irrelevant. It is not enough to prove discrimination with statistics in the abstract; a defendant must prove that the prosecutor, judge, or jury "acted with a discriminatory purpose" in his or her particular situation.

Actual Innocence. *Herrera v. Collins*, 506 U.S. 390 (1993) Herrera was convicted in 1982 of the murder of two policemen and sentenced to death. He had pled guilty to one of the murders.

His brother Raul was living at the time of the crime but died in 1984. In 1990 Herrera filed petition for relief, first in the Texas state court and then in the federal court. He claimed actual innocence and relied on four affidavits. The first was from a lawyer who had represented brother Raul in a 1984 situation. The lawyer said that Raul had told him that he, Raul, had killed the two officers. The second affidavit was from a cellmate in 1984 who said Raul had confided in him that it was he not, his brother, who had killed the two officers.

The third was from a former schoolmate who said Raul had told him one summer night in 1983 that he was the murderer, The fourth was from Raul Junior, nine years old at the time, who said he had seen his father commit the crimes.

In the appeal from the Texas court decision, the U.S. Supreme Court justices voted six to three to deny relief; the claims under "the cruel and unusual punishment" and "due process" clauses had come too late. Texas required that motions for relief based on newly discovered evidence "be made within thirty days of imposition of sentence." Therefore, the Court's refusal to entertain new evidence eight years after Herrera's conviction did not "transgress a principle of fundamental fairness." A survey of state laws had shown that only nine states had no time limits on the filing of such motions.

As for denial of relief in the lower federal courts: The Supreme Court said that justices "do not sit to correct errors of fact (guilt or innocence) but to ensure that individuals are not imprisoned in violation of the Constitution....Claims of actual innocence based on newly discovered evidence have never been held to state a ground for federal habeas relief absent an independent constitutional violation" during the original criminal proceedings.

The only possible remedy for Herrera, concluded the Court, was to request executive clemency from the governor. The justices were obviously troubled with the decision. Chief Justice Rehnquist, who wrote the opinion, acknowledged the "elemental appeal" of Herrera's contention that the Constitution prohibits execution of innocent persons. Justice O'Connor said that she could not "disagree with the fundamental legal principle that executing the innocent is inconsistent with the Constitution," but a jury had ruled that Herrera was guilty and his new evidence "is bereft of credibility." Justice Kennedy joined in O'Connor's concurring opinion.

Justice White assumed that "a persuasive showing of actual innocence made after trial, even though made after the expiration of the time provided by law for the presentation of newly discovered evidence, would render unconstitutional the execution of the petitioner in this case." But he added, the newly discovered evidence must prove that "no rational trier of fact could find proof of guilt beyond a reasonable doubt," and Herrera's affidavits "fall short of satisfying this standard."

Justice Blackmun wrote that "execution of an innocent person is at odds with contemporary standards of fairness and decency" under the Eighth Amendment and "equally offensive to the Due Process Clause of the Fourteenth Amendment." The showing required to obtain relief on a claim of actual innocence, he wrote, is proof by the petitioner "that he probably is innocent;" it would not be enough to raise doubt about his guilt. Blackmun would send the case back to the District Court to consider the issue. Justices Stevens and Souter concurred.

Justice Scalia voted with the majority because, he said, there is nothing in the Constitution that gives a right to "demand judicial consideration of newly discovered evidence brought forward after conviction." Justice Thomas agreed.

The Future. *Callins v. Collins*, 544 U.S. 2957 (1994) When the court refused to review a Texas death sentence, Justice Blackmun wrote a long and tortured dissent:

> From this day forward I no longer shall tinker with the machinery of death. For twenty years I have endeavored, along with a majority of this Court to develop procedural and substantive rules that would lend more than the mere appearance of fairness to the death penalty. Twenty years have passed since this Court declared the death penalty must be imposed fairly, and with reasonable consistency, or not at all (See *Furman v. Georgia*),

and despite the effort of the States and courts to devise formulas and procedural rules to meet this daunting challenge, the death penalty remains fraught with arbitrariness, discrimination, caprice, and mistake.

Perhaps one day this Court will develop procedural rules or verbal formulas that actually will provide consistency, fairness, and reliability in a capital- sentencing scheme. I am not optimistic that such a day will come. I am more optimistic, though, that the Court eventually will conclude that the effort to eliminate arbitrariness while preserving fairness in the infliction of death is so plainly doomed to failure that it — and the death penalty — must be abandoned altogether. I may not live to see that day, but I have faith that eventually it will arrive. The path this Court had chosen lessens us all. I dissent.

APPENDIX

THE ABA TAKES A STAND

On February 3, 1997, the House of Delegates of the American Bar Association called for a moratorium on the death penalty in the United States. Such a moratorium should continue, the ABA argued, until each jurisdiction "implements policies and procedures...to (1) ensure that death penalty cases are administered fairly and impartially, in accordance with due process, and (2) minimize the risk that innocent persons may be executed."

The ABA's resolution identified four specific areas in which the penalty as now administered falls short:

A. Competency of counsel. The ABA cited the failure of many states to implement a working public defender program and found that in most cases "grossly unqualified and undercompensated lawyers who have nothing like the support necessary to mount an adequate defense are often appointed to represent capital clients."

B. Weaknesses in the system of habeas corpus. The ABA expressed concern that state Death Row prisoners were being denied, by legislation and judicial ruling, their proper right to appeal to state and federal courts.

C. Discrimination on the basis of race. The ABA echoed Justice Harry Blackmun's concern that the death penalty was fraught with "the biases and prejudices that infect society generally." It called for executions to cease until effective mechanisms are developed to eliminate the corrosive effects of racial prejudice in capital cases.

D. Execution of the mentally retarded and persons under the age of eighteen. The House of Delegates re-affirmed existing ABA policies against the execution of mentally retarded people (adopted February, 1989) and people under the age of eighteen at the time of their offenses (adopted August, 1983), although such executions have been ruled constitutional by the U. S. Supreme Court.

On May 20, 1999, Nebraska became the first state in the Union to ratify the ABA resolution. By a count of 27 to 21, its unicameral legislature voted to declare a moratorium on executions for two years, authorizing a study to see what if anything might be done to ensure fair administration of capital cases.

By June 15, officials in two towns in the North Carolina triangle had acted similarly. Carrboro's Board of Aldermen and Chapel Hill's Town Council both passed unanimous resolutions asking Governor Jim Hunt, the state legislature, and the federal government to suspend executions until steps had been taken to guarantee that the death penalty could be imposed fairly and impartially. Their actions came less than a month after a superior court judge overturned the conviction of Charles Munsey, who had been found guilty of first-degree murder in 1996. (The judge ruled that the prosecution had concealed exculpatory evidence, that another man's confession of the crime was credible, and that the evidence indicated Munsey's innocence.)

Some Facts for Advocates

*As of January 1999, more than 5,000 men, women, and children had been sentenced to death since the Supreme Court upheld the death penalty in 1976. The 500th execution during this period occurred in South Carolina on December 18, 1998.

* Only one out of a hundred first-degree murderers is sentenced to death, and even fewer are executed.

*At any one time in the U. S., more than half the people on Death Row are African Americans. The General Accounting Office reports: "Our synthesis of twenty-eight studies shows a pattern of evidence indicating racial disparities in the charging, sentencing, and imposition of the death penalty; the race of the victim was found in all stages of the criminal justice process to have significant influence." Between 1972 and 1990, 84 percent of those put to death in this country had been convicted of killing white persons, despite the fact that almost half of all homicide victims during that same period were African Americans.

* In April, 1998, the 53-member United Nations Commission on Human Rights adopted for the second straight year a motion calling for an invalidation of capital punishment and a worldwide moratorium on executions. Reporting to the Commission's annual convention in Geneva, a special investigative panel reported that whereas executions were declining elsewhere, they were on the rise in the United States, even among juvenile defendants, the mentally impaired, and women. In response, the U. S. State Department called the report inaccurate and unfair and said "it fails to recognize properly

our extensive safeguards and strict adherence to due process."

* The Federal Bureau of Investigation reports in its publication *Crime in the United States* that murder rates in states without the death penalty average 5.1 murders per 100,000 population; states still using the death penalty average 9.1 murders.

* In every major opinion survey conducted since 1976, two-thirds or more of all Americans have endorsed the death penalty for murderers. Yet, fewer than 50 percent of the American people support the death penalty when life without parole is given as an option.

*Since October of 1994, North Carolina offers life without parole as the only alternative to the death penalty in capital cases.

*Every western democracy except the USA has abolished the death penalty.

*The USA was one of only six countries to execute a juvenile in the five years between 1991 and 1996. The others: Nigeria, Pakistan, Iran, Iraq, and Saudi Arabia.

* According to Amnesty International, in 1998 at least 1,625 prisoners are known to have been executed in 37 countries; 3,899 people were sentenced to death in 78 countries.

*In its motion for a moratorium, the American Bar Association cited as part of its rationale that "even when experienced and competent counsel are available in capital cases, they often are unable to render adequate service for want of essential funding to pay the costs of investigations and expert witnesses. In some rural Texas counties, an appointed attorney receives no more than $800 to represent a capital defendant." [In one celebrated Texas case, the Fifth Circuit Court of Appeals noted that an appointed attorney had received only $11.84 per hour.] Similar limits, the ABA said, are in place in other states. "In Virginia, the hourly rate for capital defense services works out to about $13. In an Alabama case, the lawyer appointed to represent a capital defendant...was allowed a total of $500 to finance his work, including any investigations and expert services needed. With that budget, it is hardly surprising that the attorney conducted no investigation at all."

* The death penalty in North Carolina dates from colonial times, when its administration was governed by English Common Law and acts of the Colonial Assembly. In 1910 the power to execute was taken away from local governments and assumed by the state. On March, 1910, Walter Morrrison, a black laborer from Robeson County, became the first North Carolinan to die in the electric chair. In 1982 the General Assembly gave Death Row inmates the option to choose death by lethal injection. In 1998 the Assembly did away with the electric chair, making lethal injection the only legal method of execution.

*In 1989 the U.S. Supreme Court cited polls showing that the majority of Americans oppposed executions of mentally retarded persons. Nevertheless, it left to the states the right to authorize or bar them. North Carolina has no law protecting its retarded citizens from the death penalty.

*On record for abolition of the death penalty are the senior-most leaders in fifteen religious denominations in North Carolina: African Methodist Episcopal Zion, General Baptist, Christian Methodist Episcopal, Christian Church (Disciples of Christ), Episcopal Diocese of Raleigh, Episcopal Diocese of Western North Carolina, Evangelical Lutheran Church in America, Lutheran Church Missouri Synod,

Moravian Church in America, Presbyterian Church (USA), Religious Society of Friends, Roman Catholic Dioceses of Charlotte and Raleigh, United Church of Christ, United Methodist Church, and the Universal Fellowship of Metropolitan Community Churches. Various Hebrew and Baptist congregations have adopted a similar position.

"An Eye for an Eye?"

All mainline Christian denominations are on record opposing capital punishment. Still, the myth persists that by sanctioning "an eye for an eye" the Bible is calling for the death sentence.

Take a careful look. The same Mosaic laws (to be found principally in Exodus XXI and Deuteronomy XIX) that are all too commonly assumed to condone capital punishment also call for death if a person hits or curses his/her parents, keeps an ox known to gore people, or participates in sorcery, bestiality, idolatry, or adultery. Among other crimes that the Old Testament says justify the death sentence are gluttony, disobedience, and drunkeness.

Were the death penalty applied in all these presumably warranted circumstances, we'd have few people left standing to impose the punishment.

In truth, the Hebrew text, "An eye for an eye, a tooth for a tooth," was meant to prohibit mass killings of clans out of vindictiveness. Prior to introduction of this law, the practice had been for the family of a murdered relative to exact retaliation on entire families or tribes. "An eye for an eye" meant that people could not take more than one life for a life, even if the person who was murdered was pregnant and about to give birth.

In practice, the death penalty was even further limited. It was used only on testimony of at least two persons who saw the murder about to take place and who informed the would-be murderer that he would receive the death penalty if he (or she) went through with it. If, after that warning, the person proceeded in a premeditated fashion, then and only then could the death penalty be used. Because of these restraints, the death penalty was rarely, if ever, applied in Hebrew culture.

Christian scripture added another dimension. People supporting the execution had to be sinless, and sinlessless meant not merely never to have committed murder but never to have held hate or anger in one's heart — *never*. Those who interpreted "eye for an eye" as permission for vengeance were told to forgive their enemies and to bless those who had harmed them.

In general, the death penalty flies in the face of the Chistian message that all are to be forgiven and all are redeemable.

Adapted from a statement by Leigh Eason.
The Journal of Common Sense, summer 1996.

FOR MORE INFORMATION

Books

The Death Penalty: an Historical and Theological Survey. James J. Megiven, Herald Press. 1997.

The Death Penalty and Racial Bias: Overturning Supreme Court Assumptions. Gregory D. Russell.

The Death Penalty in America: Current Controversies. Hugo A. Bedau, Editor. Oxford University Press. 1997.

The Death Penalty (Opposing Viewpoints Digests). Gail B. Stewart. Greenhaven Press. 1998.

Dead Man Walking: An Eyewitness Account of the Death Penalty in the United States. Helen Prejean.   1996.

The Arbitrariness of the Death Penalty. Barry Nakell and Kenneth A. Hardy.   1987.

Women and the Death Penalty in the United States, 1900-1998. Kathleen A. O'Shea.   1999.

In Spite of Innocence. Michael Radelet, Hugo Adam Bedau, and Constance E. Putnam. Northeastern University Press.

Just Revenge: Cost and Consequences of the Death Penalty. Mark Constanzo. St. Martin's Press. 1998.

Against the Death Penalty: Christian and Secular Arguments Against Capital Punishment. Gardner C. Hanks. Herald Press. 1997.

Online

Cornell University's Legal Information Institute. **http://law.fsu.edu.lawtech/deathpen/sct.-dp.html**

National Coalition to Abolish the Death Penalty, 1436 U Street, NW, Washington DC, 20009. (202) 387-3890. **http://www.ncadp.org/main.html**

Amnesty International. **http://www.amnesty.org/ailib/ intcom/dp/against.htm**

The North Carolina Department of Correction. **http:/ www.doc.state.nc.us/dop/deathpenalty/first.htm**

Additional Resources in North Carolina

Center for Death Penalty Litigation.   123 West Main Street, #500. Durham, NC 27701.

North Carolinians Against the Death Penalty. 1008 Lamond Avenue, Durham, NC 27701.

People of Faith Against the Death Penalty. 157$^{1/2}$ E. Franklin Street, Suite 8, Chapel Hill, NC 27514.

"Why I'm Against the Death Penalty"

Harry A. Blackmun, Justice, U. S. Supreme Court "I feel morally and intellectually obligated simply to concede that the death penalty experiment has failed."

Eva Clayton, Representative to Congress from North Carolina's First District: "The death penalty contains hypocrisy within itself. How can we justify one killing with another killing?"

Clyde Edgerton, Author: "Any legal system claiming to represent what is most noble in a society fails when embracing and welcoming the cruelty of planned death for a member of that society."

James Exum Jr., Chief Justice Emeritus, N. C. Supreme Court: "When a state says this or that human being is not worth saving, it brutalizes the rest of us and we become a more violent society."

James E. Ferguson II, Attorney: "I continue to be baffled that we call ourselves civilized and at the same time continue to use the state's machinery of death to kill those we despise — more often than not the poor, the weak, the unpopular. There is no redeeming value in killing as a form of punishment. It is not an effective deterrent. It undermines and destroys respect for human life. It appeals to our basest instincts."

Christopher C. Fordham III, Chancellor Emeritus, UNC-CH: "I have many problems with the death penalty: the finality of inevitable mistakes, the often unfair administration of justice, the uneven access to legal expertise. Most of all, I am repelled by the concept of collective killing by the community."

Rabbi John Friedman, Judea Reform Congregation, Durham: "That we use the death penalty in America is a sign of our inability to transcend our basic inclination for revenge. There is no other rational explanation for this barbaric practice."

Harvey Gantt, Democratic Candidate for the U. S. Senate:"I have yet to read any data that suggest that by imposing the death penalty we have deterred crime or reduced the frequency of capital offenses."

Paul Hardin, Chancellor Emeritus, UNC-CH: "I support wholeheartedly the ABA's call for a moratorium on the death penalty. Indeed, I would favor its outright repeal. First, although the penalty is occasionally 'deserved,' it is unevenly, even whimsically, applied. Second, when it is mistakenly imposed upon an innocent person, the miscarriage has no possibility of cure or amelioration."

Gerald Horne, Institute of African-American Research and Sonja Haynes Stone Black Cultural Center: "In 1998, seven more countries, including Canada, the United Kingdom, and Bulgaria, moved toward complete abolition of the death penalty. This puts the total number of countries in this civilized category at sixty-seven....The United States remains in select company with China, Iran, Iraq, and the Congo. Last summer, Texas executed Joseph Stanley Faulder, a Canadian citizen, despite the fact that his government objected furiously, not least because he was never notified of his legally protected right to contact the Canadian consulate...When will this state and this nation subscribe to the most civilized norms of the global village and consign the death penalty to the scrap heap of history where it belongs?"

James Megivern, Chair, Department of Philosophy and Religion, UNC at Wilmington: "The death penalty is the ultimate act of judicial arrogance. It assumes the total infallibility and omniscience of the legal system."

Pope John Paul II: "Modern society has the means of protecting itself without definitively denying criminals the chance to reform. [The death penalty is] cruel and unnecessary, even in the case of someone who has done great evil."

Barry Saunders, columnist, News & Observer: "Wendell Flowers had a last minute reprieve from his scheduled execution, after he had already eaten his last meal: chitlins and cherry cheesecake and a bottle of Cheerwine. McQuillan, the prison spokeswoman, ran down for me the 'special meals' of some inmates who'd dined, then died. John Rook ordered a dozen hot dogs. but ate only two. Velma Barfield munched Cheese Doodles, a Kit Kat, and a Coke. Ricky Lee Sanderson had a Dolly Madison honey bun. Kermit Smith ordered four pieces of extra-crispy white-meat chicken from KFC and washed it down with a Mountain Dew. There is obviously nothing 'haute' about all these Death Row chow choices. I recently switched my position on the death penalty. I now oppose it, because it is meted out exclusively to poor people. Just look at these choices for 'last meals.' It is obvious that people, even those near death, eat what they're used to eating in life. Call me crazy, but just once I'd like to see someone facing the hot squat order up some filet mignons, duck a l'orange or lobster tail. Until then, the only thing I want to see get fried is chicken."

Rev. Robert Seymour, Pastor Emeritus, Brinkley Baptist Church, Chapel Hill: "Life is the gift of God which the state does not have the right to take away. God never gives up on anyone, and nobody is beyond the possibilty of redemption."

Lee Smith, Author: "The death penalty discriminates against poor people, non-white people, and all those who do not have the resources or understanding to demand their proper rights under existing law. Furthermore, it doesn't even work."

McNeill Smith, former ABA representative to Estonia: "A country cannot qualify for membership in the European Union if it practices capital punishment. Why is it that Europeans can abolish the death penalty and we can't? Why is it that the European nations have a lower incidence of homicides? Is it because we're still locked in the Wild West tradition, where shooting and killing are to be expected and we don't want to give up the title of being the most murderous country in the world?"

Wade Smith, Attorney: "To those who contend that the death penalty is a deterrent, I say that I have represented dozens of people in death penalty cases and I never heard a single one of them express the idea that they thought of the death penalty, or even had an awareness of the death penalty, before committing their crimes. To those who say the death penalty is necessary because these defendants may be set free to kill again, I say that we now have life in prison without parole; this means defendants who commit first degree murder will never, ever, be set free. And to those who say we cannot afford to keep these people in prison for life, I say that it is infinitely more expensive to put them to death; the death penalty is a horrible waste of money....The death penalty is an embarrassment. It is a failure. It is a waste of resources. It is a blight on us as a civilization."

Chuck Stone, Walter Spearman Professor, UNC-CH School of Journalism and Mass Communication: "Based on the demographics of the death penalty's unfair application, many moral and statistical arguments speak for themselves. But the strongest argument is the irreversibility of error that wrongfully takes a human life....As long as the criminal justices system is unable to wear a mantle of infallibility and as long as prison incarcerations continue to increase despite a dramatic decrease in crime, the death penalty can claim no justification."

Melvin L. Watt, Representative to Congress from North Carolina's Twelfth District: "In North Carolina, a defendant convicted of killing a white victim is four times more likely to be sentenced to death than a defendant convicted of killing a black victim. In at least seventy-five cases, defendants have been sentenced to death and later found to be innocent."*

*In the 38 death-penalty states, as of October 1, 1998, a total of 4,003 people had been sentenced to die since the U. S. Supreme Court reinstated capital punishment in 1976. Of these, 486 had been executed and 3,517 were still imprisoned on Death Row. Among those convicted, 75 had been freed when later evidence established their innocence. (Source: NAACP Legal Defense Fund and the Northwestern University School of Law.) That such miscarriages continue, see May 1999 accounts in North Carolina press of the false conviction of Charles Munsey. Also see New York Times editorial, "Innocents on Death Row," May 23, 1999.

INDEX

About the Editors

Calvin Kytle has worked as a newspaperman, as the senior public relations executive for an insurance company, as deputy director of a federal civil rights agency, and as a Washington, D.C. communications consultant. In retirement, he thinks of himself primarily as a writer and publisher. During the fifties and sixties he was an irregular contributor to such magazines as *Coronet, Saturday Review, and Harper's*. He is the author of *Gandhi, Soldier of Nonviolence*, a biography for young people, and co-author (with former congressman James A. Mackay) of *Who Runs Georgia?*. In 1976 he founded Seven Locks Press, a small Washington-based publisher of nonfiction, mainly in the fields of public policy, politics, health, and race relations. Shortly after selling the Press in 1987, he moved with his wife, Elizabeth, to Carolina Meadows, a continuing care retirement community in Chapel Hill. Mrs. Kytle is the author of *Willie Mae*, the first-person biography of a black woman that was hailed as a "minor classic" when it appeared in 1958 and is currently in its fifth edition (paperback, the University of Georgia Press).

Daniel H. Pollitt is now an emeritus professor of constitutional law, having retired in 1992 after thirty-seven years in the UNC Law School. He was in private practice in Washington for many years after World War II, principally as an associate of Joseph Rauh, the celebrated advocacy lawyer who helped Eleanor Roosevelt found Americans for Democratic Action. While a member of the UNC faculty, Professor Pollitt frequently left the classroom to serve as defense attorney in capital cases and to represent clients among the poor, disfranchised, and disabled on issues of free speech and civil liberties. For years he has spent his summers as a special counsel to the U.S. House Committee on Education and Labor. He has been a member of the governing group of the Southern Regional Council, president of the North Carolina branch of the American Civil Liberties Union, and a member of ACLU's national board. At UNC he served four years as elected chair of the faculty. He has also served as both president of the UNC chapter of the American Association of University Professors and a representative from the Southeast on AUUP's national board.

---

*"Revenge is a kind of wild justice,
which the more man's nature runs to,
the more ought law to weed it out."*

Francis Bacon, 1625

The cover photos are of Cyrus B. King (front)
and Brandon Hill (back),
taken during a protest march in Raleigh.